*The Complete Book of Flower Preservation*

# The Complete Book of Flower Preservation

## By
## Geneal Condon

Black and white photography by Hal Rumel and Marvin Boyer
Color photography by Ed Hunt and Boyd Hill

ISBN 0–13–156802–7
      0–13–156794–2 pbk.

Library of Congress Catalog Card Number: 70–117008
Printed in the United States of America
Prentice-Hall International, Inc., London
Prentice-Hall of Australia, Pty. Itd., Sydney
Prentice-Hall of Canada, Ltd., Toronto
Prentice-Hall of India Private Ltd., New Delhi
Prentice-Hall of Japan, Inc., Tokyo

*Design by Janet Anderson*

10 9 8

*To the memory of my husband,*
*whose understanding and encouragement*
*made this work possible*

# Foreword

*I remember when the dream was very young. Geneal Condon had returned to America after several years in India and Greece. She had watched with pain as the profusion of exquisite blossoms she found there were lost forever as nature performed her rite of "bloom and fade." Flowers were, to her, creatures with souls and she was consumed with the desire to preserve as many as she could, wherever she found them. She had heard in India and learned in reading ancient books on the subject that roses were often buried in sand to retain their beauty.*

*At her home in Salt Lake City she prepared a garden. When the first flowers were ready she ordered a load of sand from a commercial sand and gravel company. She put a lilac bloom in a cardboard carton, literally poured on the sand, and waited. After several days she removed the lilac from the box. It was crushed and distorted, but a few tiny florets deep against the branch had kept their form and color. "Ah! This may not be the way but it is the direction," she thought with a glimmer of encouragement.*

*With the dedication of a scientist she pursued one method after another, and many media for drying. When she needed more sand she went to the next most obvious place, the shores of the Great Salt Lake. She found joyfully and quite by accident that for some reason this sand drew the moisture from the flowers quickly and with only an infinitely small amount of disfiguration. She was another step on the way, but she kept on, seeking the right answers.*

*Not very many people thought that what Geneal Condon was doing would develop into anything. Dried flowers? Why they, or facsimiles, could be bought any day almost anywhere! She often had the feeling that people thought she was "a wee bit touched."*

*Overcoming the handicaps of poor soil and an arid climate, she continued to nurture her garden, preserving everything it produced. Her neighbors wondered why her garden was almost constantly devoid of flowers. This was because as each blossom reached its most perfect stage, and not an instant later, it was picked and made ready for the preservation process.*

*At dawn she was tending the garden, in the afternoon she was putting the hardened blooms into containers and patiently dribbling fine lines of sand around and into the layers of petals in a kind of "reverse sculpture," building the sand up from the bottom for support as she covered each flower. In the evening she was again in the garden, touching, analyzing, questioning: "Why is the texture of one flower so much different from another? Why are their responses to treatment so different? Why is one tough and another fragile? Why do some keep their colors and others do not?" Each blossom presented an individual problem.*

*Like most dreams this was becoming a consuming thing, one of unsolved mysteries. The more she studied, the more challenging it became and the more necessary it was to understand all that her flowers could tell her. She carried sand up and down the stairs from her basement laboratory, ten, twenty, forty pounds at a time, many times a day. Some flowers were put in the sun, some dried in the oven, and some left in the normal temperature of the basement.*

*Each year she discovered more about her protégés: how to keep a perfect edge on a rose petal, when to add the shading that invariably disappeared in certain flowers, what to do with the long fragile stamens of lilies and the short compact ones of cacti, and how to combat the effects of humidity after the flowers were dried. She learned the peculiarities, temperaments and characteristics of hundreds and hundreds of plants from the root-tips up.*

*She said to each flower, "I won't let you go." She had faith in them and felt that the art she was creating was for posterity. It is a real art because, like any other, it is concerned with beauty. "Love of beauty is first," Mrs. Condon says, "and then comes self-imposed discipline." Knowing her process, or more accurately this way of life, carries one into any branch of art.*

*She had no precedent to follow, no one to whom she could turn for answers. It was hers alone. The magic that she knew was there was elusive. Discouragement had to be overcome with courage. Now she feels that she has learned "a little bit about flowers." In her book she gives you this gift, her years of work, the knowledge of one of the most beautiful experiences in life, and the method to accomplish it.*

*Elizabeth Cole*
*Perfumer*

# Contents

Foreword     vii

Flowers That Defy the Seasons     1

Flower Preservation: Benefits and Uses     8

Methods of Preserving Flowers     18

Considerations in Choosing a Method     27

The Sand Method: Preparation     33

Containers     39

Selecting the Flowers to Be Preserved     45

Dyeing Preserved Flowers     53

Covering the Flower     62

Uncovering and Cleaning the Flower     76

How to Prepare Stems     88

Ways to Preserve Foliage     96

Invade the Kitchen Garden     107

Wild Material     114

Flower Sculpture     143

The Arrangement     153

Teachers' Manual     163

Encyclopedia of Flowers and Their Special
    Treatment     175

A Parting Word     201

Index     203

*The Complete Book of Flower Preservation*

# CHAPTER I

# Flowers That
# Defy the Seasons

Among peoples all over the earth, flowers are a favorite sacrificial offering to the gods. But they die, and their beauty dies with them, on the sacrificial altar.

One of the most beautiful religious flower-legends comes from the ancient Aztecs. It is about the Lily of Mictlan (our lily of the valley) and among lilies the loveliest in the world.

Long ago, says the legend, when the gods made all earthly flowers, they had a special fondness for the lily. So they decided to make a silver lily for the gardens of heaven. Since they wanted it to be the loveliest of all lilies, they decided to form it of a tear, the most delicate of all delicate things. The gods knew that every night, in her heavenly palace, the goddess Xochiquetzel wept in her dreams, longing for the young Sun-god, so they sent the bat to steal one of her tears while she slumbered. The bat fluttered to her couch, stole the tear and flew back with it to the other gods. Then they used their magic and turned the tear—the most delicate of all delicate things—into a lily, and gave the lily the gift of eternal bloom.

But, alas, the lily they had made was gray as ashes, without color and without fragrance. And from Mictlan, the place of the departed, the laughter of Teculi, Lord of the Nether World, rose to the skies. "How can your lily be loveliest of all," he cried, "when I have had no hand in making it? Without my aid, nothing gains perfect beauty."

The gods then gave the ash-gray colorless lily to the bat and he flew down with it to Mictlan. There Teculi washed it in the waters of the river of death until it gleamed white like the mountain snow and gave forth a wonderful fragrance. But when Teculi washed it in the river of death, it exchanged its gift of eternal bloom for the gift of beauty. There was no place for it in heaven because it was doomed to fade, for all its loveliness. So Teculi sent the silver lily back to earth again. And the lily took root on earth in a lagoon where rushes grew. There, for a brief season of bloom, it rises in its silver beauty, breathing a magic fragrance, and then it fades, for it is a child of another world, the property of Teculi, Lord of Mictlan, who only lends it to earth to give men a passing moment of joy.

All those things on earth which are loveliest seem to be ours for a very little time. Man, growing and loving flowers down through the ages, has wished to regain the gift of eternal bloom for their fresh and delicate beauty. He would like them to remain exactly as he sees them, to be enjoyed forever at the height of their perfection. In this desire probably originated the art of preserving flowers. Indeed, this art is as old as time. A glimpse of its early cultivation was seen in a comparatively recent excavation of a tomb of one of the Egyptian Pharoahs. When this tomb was opened, one of the first objects that caught the eyes of the workers was a bunch of dried roses on the sarcophagus.

Material remains indicate that Egyptian culture spread to nearby Crete and, undergoing native changes there, eventually reached the Greek mainland where it became Hellenized. The Romans borrowed it, added the Italian touch, then carried it with them over the then known world. What they failed to accomplish from Rome, Alexander had already done from Greece.

Embedded in this culture and traveling with it were all the arts and handicrafts of each successive civilization. Their remains in the form of marble, clay, and metal make up our history books of yesterday. Since the art of flower preserving did show up centuries later in Europe and in India, it is reasonable to suppose this "know-how" was also passed along in this passage of time. But dealing with more transient materials than metal or stone, it succumbed to the ravages of the years.

There is evidence that this art was practiced as early as the fourteenth century in India. On one occasion while I was there, a Hindu mystic, when telling me about the abundant virtues of the beautiful wife of the Shah Jehan, said: "And she had the shining sands from the sacred Ganges brought to her bower in which she buried the roses for which she was famous, so that their bloom could be made eternal." It seems logical that these early people did use the material at hand that could do the job—sand. Thus flower preserving has come down through the centuries.

In *The Cloister and the Hearth*, an historical romance laid in fifteenth-century Europe, we read this description of yet another way of preserving roses:

So the good lassies, being questioned close, did let me know the rosebuds are cut in summer, and then laid in great clay pots, this ordered; first bay-salt, then a row of buds and over that bay-salt sprinkled; then another row of buds placed crosswise, for they say it is death to the buds to touch one another; and soon, buds and salt in layers. Then each pot is covered and soldered tight, and kept in cool cellar. And on Saturday night the master of the house, or mistress, if master be none, opens the pot and doles out the rosebuds to every female in the house, high or low, withouten a grudge, and then solders it up again. And such of these buds would full blown roses make, put them in warm water a little space, or else in the stove, and then with a tiny brush and soft, wetted in Rhenish wine, do coax them till they ope their folds. And some perfume them with rose-water. For alack! their smell is fled with the summer, and only their fair bodies lie withouten soul in tomb of clay, awaiting resurrection.

‡‡ 3 ‡‡

Preserved flowers decorated the finer homes in colonial America; and the art of preserving was well known in Victorian times. In fact it was the mention of a process of preserving flowers in an old Victorian cookbook that first interested me in the art. I was browsing through the book, which belonged to my mother—one of those tomes that always devoted a chapter or two to miscellaneous information—and somewhere between a recipe for removing warts and details on how to take grass stains out of linen was this bit of information: "Fresh flowers buried in sand for two weeks will become permanent and retain their color and form." That was all.

Being busy at the time with two small children, I felt I had no time to play with sand and flowers. But I stored the information away in my mind, and a few years later I was able to put it to a test in Athens, Greece, where my husband was in government service. The wife of our ambassador to Greece was organizing the Cavalcade of Greek Fashions to stimulate and publicize native products and talents. It was to be shown in Athens, Paris, New York, Washington, Los Angeles and elsewhere in the United States. Since I had made actual and imitation flower jewelry out of seeds (and some of my products exhibited in Paris), I was asked to create some flower jewelry to be worn with the gowns. It was then that I recalled what I had read years before about preserving flowers.

My first real experiment with blooms was with the buds of the pink almond, grown so profusely in Greece. It worked—after a fashion—but the results certainly were not comparable to what I am now able to do. Very effectively, I combined the preserved buds with the full-blown blossoms made of synthetic material. Then, emboldened by my success, I started in on other garden varieties and with all sorts of blossoms.

With each succeeding attempt, I learned something new. I compared notes with gardeners, botanists and chemists. I picked up new techniques from each of these experiences. I devoted one full summer to research work at the Library of Congress, picking out bits and pieces of pertinent information on the historical background of this art, along with useful hints on how to perfect it. However, I really did not get down to the hard core of preserving flowers until 1953, after we had returned to Utah from a stay in India and Pakistan. I have been experimenting ever since, learning and applying the knowledge I acquired in other lands and discovering new techniques.

What I have been doing—and what I hope you will be able to do after reading this book—is to bring the spring and summer and fall indoors intact, so that come those urgent stormy nights during the three or four bleak months of winter, you really will have June in January. It is always glowingly satisfying, of course, to gaze upon a lovely summer garden of blooming plants and shrubs. But it is even more thrilling to come into the house out of wintry snows and winds and find rooms aglow with the beauties of a dozen or more varieties of flowers.

Flowers—lilacs, peonies, bachelor's buttons, water lilies, roses, hollyhocks, delphiniums—almost every flower that decorates gardens and pools can be all about you as they always are about me, in their natural color and beauty, with not a petal out of place, not a bit of foliage disturbed, the stems as green as when they were growing in the garden. I am speaking of my incredibly lifelike flowers, as did the man who came to my front door one snowy, blustery day, rang the bell, and said: "Ma'am, I just want to ask you one question. Are they real?"

I knew what he meant, of course, but simply had to ask: "Are what real?" "Those flowers in your window," he said pointing to a large display of Rosa hugonis, bridal wreath, yellow marigolds and white daisies I had placed in the window facing the street to the north. He came inside and when he saw twenty or thirty similar arrangements, made with nearly forty varieties of blooms, he became excited. He discovered they were real. "Oh, they're dried, aren't they?" he asked, and right there was when I set him straight. "No," I replied, "they are not dried. They are preserved."

This, to me, is quite a different thing and is accomplished by various processes, including the use of basic desiccants. The difference—and this has been the consensus of all who have come to see and admire—between the ordinary "dried" flower and the properly preserved bloom is the same difference as that between a mail order dress and the Paris original.

‡‡ 5 ‡‡

So this is not a book about dried flowers, a term which always suggests to me those conglomerate masses of dried weeds, pods and everlastings that so many women now, as in grandmother's day, gather and arrange into a "bouquet." These materials require little or no preparation for most of them can simply be hung upside down. The atmosphere does the rest. But do not misunderstand me. I do not disparage this type of material. It has its proper place—not used exclusively by itself—but combined with other interesting and more exacting materials to bring out the life of the entire composition. Proper attention will be given to them as we proceed with the consideration of all plant material.

What I set out to do is to take a fresh garden flower, picked only minutes before being put through the process, and preserve it so that every line, every graceful curve, every stamen remains in all its natural loveliness, and with all the tints and shadows still aglow in their original splendor.

How long will they last? If you take care of them, preserved flowers will last indefinitely. They do not like strong sunlight; it fades them. Do not move them from house to house when there is a wind or when it is raining. They do not mind extreme heat or cold providing the atmosphere is dry and calm. They resent exposure to high humidity unless they are properly sprayed with a moisture-proofing spray. And they protest against people whose pinching fingers break their petals. You must instruct your guests to "admire" but not to "touch." In other words they want to be left alone, and if they are, they will give a good account of themselves. Some of my customers have enjoyed their flowers for as long as ten years; others replace them every year.

Learning the art of flower preservation has taken years of painstaking work, but I hope that through the medium of this book I can eliminate much of that hard work for you. It is a challenging work. It will be found heartbreaking at times. It requires the absolute limit of patience. You will find, as I have, that flowers are individuals and that each bloom, like each child has its own personality. You may cut two identical blooms from the same branch with no apparent difference in the flowers.

Yet, under treatment, one will act like a spoiled brat, the other like an angel.

Every year more and more scientific work is being done on plants to determine their natures, habits, and what, if any, characteristics they possess that make them akin to people. Some scientists have long held the theory that they speak a language of their own. Others say that they react visibly to noise and vibrations of different intensities. One of the recipients of the 1969 Nobel Prize for Medicine, Dr. Max Delbruck, professor of biology at the California Institute of Technology in Pasadena, California, has stated that he is no longer working in his former field. He is now investigating the "seeing eyes" of plants such as bean shoots, which enable them to twist and grow toward the light.

My own homespun experience, based only on observation, has been that, like children, plants are responsive to love, praise and discipline.

Almost any flower can be preserved, yet the garden still has some hard-headed ones, which I will discuss later. But in spite of these exceptions, one's summer garden is still a gold mine. And Nature is such a spendthrift that no one person could ever hope to preserve all of the lavish treasures that come from one little packet of seeds. New conquests are being made every day. Now, even their elusive fragrance can be recaptured. No longer do flower preservers need to recall the lament in *The Cloister and the Hearth* that, "Only their fair bodies lie withouten soul in tomb of clay, awaiting resurrection." The creative genius of today has been able to restore even this.

But I envision more. Every day I spend in trying to perfect the preserving process teaches me that flower preservation can proudly take its place with the other fine arts. It begins as a hobby and it can also end there with all of the satisfaction and fun to be obtained from similar projects. But it need not end there. It can lead into the creative field of true artistry. To lift it from the "busy work" category into the creative field is my ultimate aim. To reveal to each participant the unequaled joy in striving for perfection instead of being satisfied with mediocrity is my goal. It is what I have tried to instill in my pupils.

# 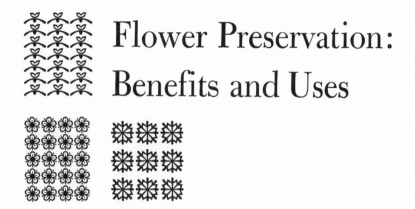 Flower Preservation: Benefits and Uses

"Thank you, Mrs. Condon, for creating so much beauty in this too often ugly world." Thus, one of the editors of *The Readers' Digest* wrote me several years ago.

Since then our world has continued to grow uglier day by day and year after year. Each of us needs an escape from the sordid happenings which we hear about and see every day. But merely to hide our heads in the sand, like the proverbial ostrich, is not the answer. How much better to spend this recuperative time, our moments of escape, in trying to replace some of the tranquility and beauty that has been taken out of our everyday lives. We owe such an effort both to ourselves and our world.

A hobby of some form is a constructive answer. But to be truly worth our consideration and time, it should have a creative purpose. There are many different types of worthwhile projects, and while I am not advocating flower preservation for everyone, I would like to point out some of its particular attractions. I doubt if there are many hobbies that touch such a variety of challenging fields: gardening (which could include hybridizing and landscaping), chemistry, designing, botany, physics, flower arranging and more.

I would begin with its value to the home, because whatever enriches these surroundings is bound to be reflected in the life of its members. Then what better way to share a sense of beauty than around a well-appointed dining table, graced with a beautiful bouquet of flowers that can be enjoyed every day of the year without withering and looking faded? And what member of the family would not be responsive to a dramatic sweep of summer blossoms in the living room during the dark and dismal days of winter? There are so many ways to use them that you will wonder how you ever got along without them. This sharing of their charm can be extended to your friends as well. They, too, will be delighted with their beauty when they come to call and I know of no better way to convey that warmth of friendship than by a gift of them to a friend, especially to those people (whom we all know) who "have everything."

The therapeutic value of this hobby is unmistakable. I have noted the soothing power this work has had on various of my pupils, from eight to eighty. The effects of daily frustrations are clearly evident in their looks and behavior when they arrive for class. Before long, however, as they become engrossed in the work, these effects disappear. One pupil put it this way: "I don't have time to worry when I'm doing this."

The substantiation of this theory was brought to my attention in an article that I recently read in a national magazine. It stated that executives, bank presidents, and heads of large corporations are now having sandboxes installed in their offices. They have found that during the stress and strain of their busy days, a few minutes of relaxation, just running their hands through the sand, clears their thinking and refreshes them for the problems ahead. They have even gone so far as to turn the sandbox into a thing of beauty by having it made of imported marble, mosaics and rare woods. Some even import colored sand to add to its attractiveness. An imposing collection of photographs accompanied the article.

All this is fine, but I would go further by suggesting that these same people have a less impressive supply of this same material (a later chapter will explain why I recommend the sand method of flower preservation) on hand in their homes so that after the day's work is done they can clear their minds of the day's problems with the same type of therapy, but with a creative purpose in mind. The search for a little beauty while they are relaxing would complete the treatment. And indeed, I have been asked to conduct a class for doctors who perhaps need to "get away from it all" more than anyone else.

I can think of no better hobby for semi-invalids, shut-ins and elderly people. Flower preservation not only can be done in a relatively small area and with comparatively few materials, but it also touches on the nostalgic things—gardening, flower arranging and more. It has been suggested that this work be introduced in geriatric wards of some hospitals and rest homes. Even though the patient is confined to his bed or wheelchair, a small table plus his working materials can bring hours of interest and pleasure every day.

I have had pupils brought to me who were suffering from mental disturbances of various kinds and who, I was later told, were greatly improved after finishing the course. In some instances, arthritic people were able to greatly improve the dexterity of their hands and fingers by working in this sand. Note well that this is the sand method of which I am speaking, not others. For instance, I should hesitate to attribute the same curative qualities to the use of cornmeal and borax. Indeed, I find borax not only annoying but I question the hygienic wisdom of using it, because it always produces a film that gets on clothing, skin and hair, and it is constantly being inhaled while working with it. On the other hand, it has long been suggested that the briny waters of Great Salt Lake have curative values. Indeed, I have received several requests from medical scientists requesting samples of the sand and water for tests. One pupil who registered for the class momentarily forgot that she had been afflicted with eczema on her hands and arms since birth. When she saw that she was required to work in the sand with her hands, she said, "Oh, I can't do that. The sand would irritate my hands and make them worse." Then moments later, "Oh, let me try it anyway. It looks like so much fun." A week later when she came to class she exclained, "Look! my hands are all clear! They have never been like that before!" The eczema did not return.

Flower preserving promotes a new awareness of the great outdoors. The advocate of this hobby learns to SEE, not just to

LOOK at nature. As he searches through the countryside for material, he discovers a completely new world of variety and detail of which up until now he may have been unaware.

Although the primary purpose of the pursuit of flower preservation is the challenge to create a satisfying work of beauty, and because of this it can and should be classed with the fine arts, yet, its monetary potentials can also be considered. There are many and they range from big business to pin money. Williamsburg, Virginia, has been conducting a brisk business in selling dried flowers for many years. I say dried flowers advisedly because they employ the hang and dry method, for historical reasons. Therefore, many of their products do not have the fresh look that other methods provide, yet they sell a great many of them. Less ambitious possibilities could include classes that can be organized, taught by experienced and competent pupils, and yield a profit. Some exclusive gift shops welcome the right to sell the flowers on consignment. Individual customers will often pay well for an arrangement designed for a special room. Working with interior decorators has amounted to a substantial profit for me, because so very often they need "that certain touch for a certain room." Local museums and historical societies will often welcome a collection of the "real thing," in lieu of the plastic or pressed varieties. They can be offered for sale in church bazaars or antique shows. Other possibilities include preserved flowers in shadow boxes, arrangements under glass bells (I recently did one of the latter for the Church of the Latter-Day Saints), decorated candlesticks, and so forth. Many of these uses will be considered in the next chapter and it would not be amiss to consider them with an eye to their commercial potential as well as for your own use.

While preserved flowers are used primarily as bouquets for the home, they may be put to a great many more uses. They make unique gifts because what nicer way to say "Happy Birthday" or "Merry Christmas" than a permanent arrangement of summer flowers when cold January winds howl outside and the countryside is covered with ice and snow? Even if the receiver of your gift "has everything," chances are he does not have nor ever has had preserved flowers.

A bouquet of preserved flowers makes an excellent gift for the sick for it can be enjoyed in the home or in the hospital with no danger from pollen or heavy perfume. Furthermore, they need not be watered and may be taken home with the patient. Having no pollen, they are a boon to hay fever sufferers.

They also make excellent Christmas and special holiday decorations. One advantage of such flowers and foliage is that they can be prepared far in advance so that you can avoid the last great rush. Table arrangements, garlands, wreaths and fruit bowls take on a new interest made from or even combined with this fascinating material. The beloved Christmas holly can be preserved and used all through the Christmas holidays and then stored away and brought out year after year while still retaining its fresh look. I did an arrangement of it last year for a local jewelry store. I combined it with a series of thin red tapers, to match the berries. It proved sensational (because it did not curl up and fade as holly always does after several days), yet the holly I used was four years old. In my classes we have done numerous wreaths, swags and garlands, all of evergreen material that has been preserved and decorated with other preserved material such as miniature fruits, pine cones, seed pods, and even flowers. They were outstanding in originality and could be used for many years with no sign of deterioration. Some pupils even preserved small Christmas trees in their entirety that were equally durable. The proverbial Christmas bowl of fruit takes on a new look with sprigs of preserved foliage and an appropriate flower or two tucked in here and there.

Wild roses in a pale green velvet frame.

Who but the very rich could afford to decorate candlesticks and candelabra with fresh red roses, which, without water, would last but a few hours at best? You can, with the material you will prepare in advance and they will last as long as you want them to. Equally interesting decorations can be made for other holidays and special events throughout the year, with your own inspiration and imagination as your guide.

How often have you grown a perfect flower and as you admired its fleeting beauty wished you could keep it forever? You can do just that! When you have preserved it, mount it on a background of velvet and this, properly framed, makes a charming wall piece. Or you may wish to use a flower that has been treated with the new "Flower Sculpture Formula," which is a preserved flower that has been specially treated so that it is not only more durable, but resembles a piece of fine porcelain, still retaining the grace and beauty it had when growing in the garden. I have done a great many such pieces, both large and small, including reed mats, framed miniatures, hanging baskets, shadow boxes, and so forth.

Several years ago, I purchased a piece of heavy mesh wire called "hardware cloth," obtainable at any hardware store. I had it cut about two feet wide and four feet long. I painted it gold and, by means of wire and glue, mounted a sweep of pastel-colored preserved flowers and preserved foliage along its entire

Swag of pastel-colored flowers mounted on a piece of gilded hardware cloth.

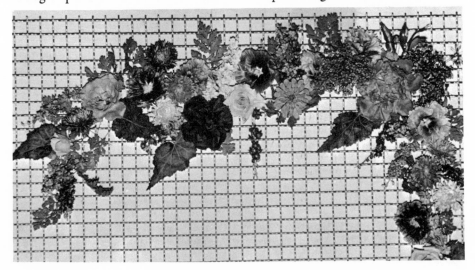

length. It was hung above a bed by velvet ribbons and for many years has made a beautiful addition to a white and gold bedroom. Later I did a smaller one which I painted Pompeian green, antiqued the finish and decorated with red floribunda roses. It proved to be a stunning color accent in a black and white dining area.

Hanging baskets of the wire mesh variety turn out to be conversation pieces when filled with airy, preserved greens and flowers of the hues that complement a certain chosen location. Shadow boxes are far more interesting when showing off real flowers instead of artificial ones. Lampshades may be trimmed with these flowers and provide the look of the "imported touch." The flowers may be left in their natural colors or may be sprayed with gold if the decor requires it.

I have often sprayed the preserved flowers and leaves with metallic paints such as gold, copper and silver, and have decorated Christmas candles with them. The process is simple; when they are ready to apply, attach the stems (which must be cut very short) to the candle with coarse thread or fine wire. The wire can be hidden by cleverly-placed leaves. Then display the candle in a bed of greenery and you have achieved a charming effect.

Wall brackets, even bird cages, take on a new life and beauty when decked with the cheerfulness of flowers instead of the usual, monotonous green. These flowers can be used with and among potted plants of live greenery and look as if they were growing there; the stems will not be bothered one bit by the water or soil.

Topiary trees, composed of any appropriate greenery, can be done for the home. This type of decoration is best made with glycerinized foliage, because foliage preserved in this manner is more pliable and is better able to withstand wear and tear. The materials you will need are: a stem of appropriate thickness and length, several styrofoam balls or cones, glue, a container to stand it in, and enough short-stemmed, preserved and sprayed foliage to completely cover the styrofoam forms when inserted with glue (the forms should be sprayed green before covering them). When they are finished, you may even shear them into any shape that you may desire. The stem may then be centered in your container and held in place with any good plastering material and allowed to dry. For a natural effect, fill the container with soil or sand. I like to cover the top of the filler with moss that has been dipped in green liquid dye and dried.

For the last few years there has been a decorating craze for ornamental flower trees for use in the home, but all of them are made with plastic leaves and flowers. I decided to make some of my own, using preserved material. My trees were made of Chinese tree peonies, one purple, one pink and one red. They are not difficult to make and are well worth the effort. First you must purchase the bare tree, which is of manzanita wood and obtainable at most garden shops. Having prepared your material, you must decide and mark where your flowers and leaves are to be attached. Now, bore holes through the branches, where your marks are, with a small-sized bore. Apply glue to the stem of each flower and leaf as you insert them in the individual holes. The finished tree may then be placed in a tub or ornamental container and anchored in the same way that I described with topiary trees. I shall never again be without one in my own home. I have even installed a floodlight to be turned on it at night. With reasonable care, the trees should last for about four or five years.

Preserved flowers also make striking party favors, place cards and corsages for that special occasion. For this, however, they must be placed in foolproof boxes or surrounded by some protective shield, such as a ruffled paper-lace or net doily. They add grace and dignity to any office, hotel or banquet room. Several years ago I did an arrangement which was placed in our state capitol. I hope some day to do another, of our state flower, the sego lily. Wouldn't it be a good idea to have the state flower of every state preserved in its capitol? Then there is the valuable museum collection that is always in demand. I did a collection of wild flowering plants (in their entirety) at the instigation of the United States Forest Service about four years ago. They were placed under glass at the Red Canyon Visitor Center, Flaming Gorge National Recreation Area, Utah, where literally thousands of visitors see them every year. They run the gamut in variety, of early spring through fall; thus the tourist can see the plants which are indigenous to that area, exactly as they grow in the wild.

In connection with wild flowers, next time you plan to enter your local flower show, why not plan to exhibit something different? Compose a wild plant grouping of preserved material that may be out of season yet appropriate to the subject and category of the show. I assure you that your display will be a sensation. However, when exhibiting in flower shows, make sure that your material is not dyed. Show it exactly as it grew. The rules of most flower shows prohibit the entrance of material that has been touched up in any way.

One of the most important uses for this preserved material is its value in the classroom. It is a well-known fact that fresh material of the wild variety wilts before it can be brought in and studied. The pressed specimens, so widely used in the past, lack the natural appearance and growth habits that are so important and distinctive a part of their characteristics. The ability to preserve plant life, from the lowest root to the topmost bud, should be a MUST in all botany classes. Indeed, it is being done. A large percentage of my correspondence has come from high school students who were taking plant preserving for their botany project. They were highly enthusiastic in their praise of its value in their work. It could very well be that the knowledge and ability to preserve plant material could prove to be the botanist's most useful assistant.

The recipes and directions for the "candying" of flowers and leaves will be given in a later chapter. These are perfectly edible and a delectable confection at that. What more novel and attractive idea for a candy or a garnish for a dessert than these delicious morsels of living flower? Once you learn to do them, your imagination will take flight; you will think of dozens of ways to use them.

Then there is the special treatment which I call the "Flower Sculpture Formula." Flowers thus treated are not edible, but a collection of them can grace the table as a centerpiece and can be used for many other decorative purposes. When properly done, their substance and durability are greatly strengthened, yet they resemble a fine piece of porcelain, still retaining all the delicacy and grace that only nature can produce. They can be safely cleaned and dusted and withstand an unbelievable amount of rough treatment. Because of this, they can be used to decorate mirrors, bottles and boxes. They can be left in their natural colors or be sprayed in the decorator's choice. When they are finished, they can be glued on whatever surface you wish. Then listen to the compliments. Here, indeed, is a major breakthrough in the flower world. However, to practice the art of flower sculpture, you must first learn the art of flower preservation because the former is built upon the latter.

This is but a bird's eye view of the possibilities of putting to practical use the products of this art. There are many more, and the inventive mind will search them out.

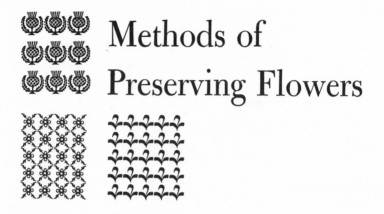

# CHAPTER III

# Methods of
# Preserving Flowers

A wave of enthusiasm for preserving flowers has swept over the United States during the last few years. Perhaps an aversion to cold, stiff, and unnatural uniformity has brought people to the conclusion that neither manufactured fiber, paraffin, nor molded plastic can ever approach the reality of nature's work.

With each new attempt comes experimentation with new drying media. Sawdust, sugar, talcum powder, cornstarch, washing powder, silica gel, borax and cornmeal, and sand are only a few of the materials claimed to be best. Superficial dabbling without clear standards and goals often leads to the misuse of such superlatives as "best," "easiest," and "quickest."

The reader is warned to beware of such catch phrases, because as yet there is no known substance that will preserve all flowers perfectly any more than there is a medicine that will cure all diseases. All have some merit, and some are better than others. But even with the best methods, some plants will not respond.

Possibly our approach has been wrong from the beginning. All the media now known and used are desiccating materials. Thus, the flower is robbed of its natural juices; only its cell structure is left. Until science comes up with a formula and method for replacing what the desiccant now removes, and as rapidly as it removes it, no flower will be perfectly preserved.

## Methods of Preserving Flowers

Let us consider the best-known and most widely used desiccating materials and compare what they do. Results will vary, of course, with the skill of the preserver and with the conditions under which the preserving is done.

Reduced to its simplest terms, the process of preserving flowers involves slowly drying out freshly cut blooms in a manner that leaves them lifelike in form, color and texture. The process can be done in one of three ways: (1) by exposing the flowers to warm dry air, (2) by embedding them for a time in a granular desiccating medium, or (3) by immersing them in a special liquid or in plastic. Of the three, only the second has proven to be generally satisfactory for preserving a wide variety of blooms in their natural freshness and it is therefore the principal concern of this book. In particular, I advocate the use of Great Salt Lake sand. Having tried and compared it with all the other media for flower drying, my conclusion, as you will see in the following chapters, is that to my knowledge it is the best desiccant for flower preservation in the world today.

To reach a conclusion such as this requires many years of flower drying. It entails constant comparisons of methods, procedures, techniques and materials. One should not rule out all other methods in favor of one which he happens to like unless he can supply valid reasons for so doing, together with convincing proof of his findings. Habits often tend to create favorites and often one will go to extreme lengths to defend a favorite. Then again, unless comprehensive comparisons are made as to the quality and degree of perfection that is obtained by a habitual way of doing something, a kind of lethargy occurs and one might be inclined to say, "Oh well, the method I am used to is good enough for me. Why should I change?" The answer, of course, is that changes are made in order to produce better products.

### The Hang and Dry Method

This method was used by the early English colonists, when flower drying began its career in America. It is still used to produce the massed bouquets seen at Monticello, Williamsburg and Mount Vernon. Its historical authenticity gives it priority over other systems even though better flowers are produced by more exacting methods. There is still some use for it among the most modern adherents of flower drying because some types of materials naturally respond in the same manner no matter what treatment you give them. Since it is so easy and simple, it will probably continue to be used for those few varieties that are not particular as to how they are treated.

Material to be dried is gathered and tied in bunches, then hung upside down in a dark, dry, warm place until the stems and flowers are stiff. Because I live in a dry climate, my workroom in the basement suffices, but for those people who live in humid areas, the basement might be too damp. In such cases an attic or clothes closet on the upper level of the house would be more satisfactory. In any case, clotheslines, hooks or clothes hangers are suitable supports while drying.

This simple process is the easiest and quickest way to preserve weeds, grasses and seed-pod collections. It can be used in the treatment of all everlasting and straw flowers. Care should be taken to cut the latter just before they come into full bloom before hanging them to dry. Contrary to some common practice, this method should NOT be used on most cultivated flowers. The following flowers are the only ones that I subject to this treatment. I have tried them by other methods and found that they did just as well dried in the open air: celosia, goldenrod, acacia, yarrow, baby's breath, sedum, cattail, heather, chives, dock, honesty, ocotillo, pussy willow, and tamarisk. The first three of the list, when hung upside down and allowed to dry, retain their velvety texture much better than when buried in a desiccant. When they are taken out of the drying agent and put through the cleaning process, you will find it difficult to remove the adhering particles of the drying material without breaking the feathery segments of the flower head. Even though this simple method is used, the necessity for the proper grooming and restoring of the material to its natural state remains. For instance these same three flowers, when preserved by the hang and dry method, have a tendency to become much too stiff looking. The flower heads become somewhat matted and ungraceful, the stems straight and rigid. You can remedy this condition by holding the dried material over the spout of a boiling teakettle. If this is done skillfully, the flower heads will puff up to their original shape and position. Stems so treated will become pliable enough to be bent in any position desired. The accompanying foliage is improved also by this treatment because it, too, in its upside down position, tends to point downward as it dries. Thus when it is reversed and placed in the arrangement, the unnatural upward direction of the leaves is corrected and they fall gracefully into place. (This is particularly true of the acacia, with its accompanying mass of gray-green foliage.) Of course, the work must be done quickly because they become set and dry almost immediately.

Everlastings, while treated this way, come under a different grouping. They are annuals that are grown from seed, and, unlike the other flowers mentioned above, have a built-in, self-sustaining characteristic of their own which becomes apparent as they reach maturity. Other than making sure that the plants are well grown and dry when cut, no other responsibility remains except to harvest them at the right stage of bloom, usually just before maturity. They are not great in number but are sometimes hard to come by in their entire range from the local garden centers. Therefore, you may have to order them. Burpee Seed Company, Philadelphia, Pennsylvania, with branches in Clinton, Iowa, and Riverside, California, lists five of them. In addition, they offer ornamental grasses, honesty and Job's tears, which can all be preserved in the same way. The classic list includes: Acroclinium, Globe amaranth, Helichrysum, Statice sinuata and Xeranthemum. An additional variety not often listed is Ammobium, a winged everlasting Australian plant with silvery white flowers and yellow centers. Vaughn Seed Company has it.

## Borax Methods

The borax-and-cornmeal and the borax-and-sand methods seem to be the favorites of most flower dryers. I have experimented with them both but my enthusiasm waxes thin when I compare their merits with their shortcomings. It is true that this method is preferable to the hang and dry procedure because it does support the drying flower and thereby preserves somewhat more of its original shape. But when the flower emerges from the desiccant a coating of borax is plainly visible on the surfaces of the petals which I find difficult, if not impossible, to remove. The individual particles of the desiccant are of irregular shape and construction and those with sharp and jagged edges have a tendency to mar and pockmark the delicate petals. Then, too, there is a danger of burning petal surfaces and edges if the flower is kept in the solution too long. This is especially true of white flowers. They emerge from the compound white, true to color, but as they stand and are exposed to the air for several weeks, telltale brown edges and marks appear. In addition, there is the inherent danger to one's health and well-being by constant exposure to the borax, which I have mentioned in a previous chapter.

However, there are those advocates who continue to use these mixtures and for their benefit, here are the standard proportions: either (1) two parts of borax to one part of white cornmeal, or (2) two parts of borax to one part of sand. The devotees of this method tell you that you can put a number of flowers in the same container and cover them with the desiccant, either face up or face down or horizontal, as the flower demands. The drying time varies, of course, but the average length of time for the interment is about two weeks, less two or three days if the sand and cornmeal combination is used. The sand to be used is any ordinary sand that has been washed, dried and sifted. The borax is obtainable at any grocery store. The name Twenty Mule Team may strike a familiar note and is the same as borax in the bulk except that it may be slightly more expensive because of packaging.

### Silica Gel

Silica gel is an agent often used to dry the air around items and substances that do not tolerate humid weather. It has been packaged, given a commercial name, and sold as a desiccant in which flowers may be preserved. This is a mixture of coarse and fine granules. The coarse grains are colored blue and they lose this hue when the compound has absorbed its capacity of moisture. Instructions on the package require the user to embed the flower in the material, seal the container with tape, and leave it alone for a week. It is then untaped, and the material poured off the flower and used over again on another. After several usings, the chemical will have absorbed its maximum capacity of water and must be dried out in the oven before it is ready to be reused.

Compared to sand or a borax mixture, this chemical is relatively expensive and this drawback alone would make it prohibitive in cost during the summer flowering season when sprays and tall stalks, such as delphinium, are blooming in profusion and literally screaming to be preserved. Therefore, unless one can limit one's desires to a relatively few specimens, the cost could very easily wreck the family budget. Then, too, as with the borax and sand, the composites are of irregular shape and contour, which will cause blemishes on the surfaces of the petals. It is a very rapid drying chemical, hence the warning not to leave the flower submerged longer than a week. The mixture even feels hot in the hand and the faster the drying action occurs, the greater the danger of burning or fading.

## *The Story of Oolitic Sand*

My favorite of all drying media is sand and the best variety comes from the shores of Great Salt Lake in Utah. Most sands are the result of erosion, the elements and time breaking down rocks into tiny particles. Consequently, their grains often have sharp ends and jagged edges which make them unsuitable for flower drying because these ends and edges tend to pierce or pockmark the petals.

Sand from Great Salt Lake, however, is a "built up" sand; it is classed as an oolitic variety. The lake from which it comes is a remnant of old Lake Bonneville which covered most of the western area at one time. Now shrunken in size and with no outlet, it is surrounded by mountains whose rich minerals have been washed through the highly mineralized waters by wave action forms nearly one-third of its content, nothing lives in the lake except the tiny salt or brine shrimp and these abound there by the trillions. The excrement and eggs of these tiny shrimp are

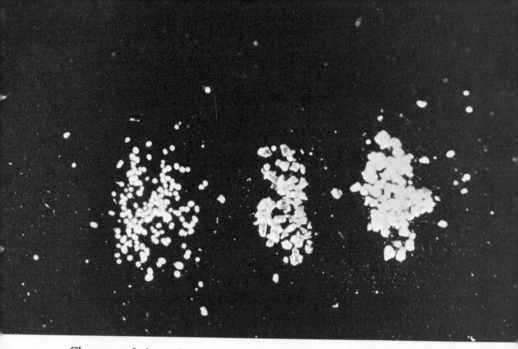

Close-up of three desiccating agents shows differences in granular texture. Oolitic sand (left) is composed of loose, globular grains. Silica gel (center) is more compact, has rougher edges. Borax sand (right) tends to stick together.

washed through the highly mineralized waters by wave action and during this process are coated with minerals and limestone in much the same way that a pearl is formed in an oyster. The minute eggs are smoothly and evenly coated, hence are deposited on the shores as uniform, tiny pellets. Eventually the eggs disintegrate, leaving each grain of sand with a soft, hollow and somewhat absorbent center. As a result the sand literally pulls the moisture out of the flower and holds it until it evaporates.

Consisting mostly of limestone, this sand is considerably heavier than other varieties, such as the silica type. This additional weight has proved to be of considerable importance as will be shown in a later chapter.

Since Great Salt Lake sand is highly mineralized, it may also contain certain chemical substances which help in the drying process. I have found that its alkaline content is responsible for the true preservation of many colors, such as blues, lavenders and purples.

When I first started using this sand (some eighteen years ago), it was available only to the people living in this area. Now I am glad to report that this sand, already washed, sifted and bagged can be obtained in any quantity. A self-addressed and stamped postcard mailed to Flowers and Crafts, Heritage Square, Golden, Colorado 80401, will supply the needed information.

Because there are always those people who do not want to go to the trouble of acquiring the original and who would rather make do with what they have, I have developed a formula which is simple and inexpensive and is a substitute for Great Salt Lake sand. When employed in conjunction with ordinary sand—either river, beach or desert—it produces a synthetic drying medium which, when properly used, will give *nearly* the same results as oolitic sand. Complete directions for preparing the formula will be given in a later chapter.

### Activated Alumina

There are times in early spring when the first roses are ready, or in the fall, when chrysanthemums are at their peak, that I may wish for a more powerful drying action than is ordinarily required. At such times I use Activated Alumina, a product of Alcoa. The coarse bits are about the size of a pea and are many times more powerful than silica gel as a desiccant. I use about one tablespoonful to a container of sand. Of course I never allow any of the alumina particles to come in contact with the flower itself. After the flower is covered, I gently press some of the grains in the sand away from the flower and end by sprinkling some on top. In this way they cannot injure the flower but do assist the sand in its process of desiccation. Since they are rather large in size they can easily be sifted out before the sand is re-used. I recommend this procedure ONLY during inclement weather and ONLY on very double flowers whose centers, though apparently dry, still contain an unusual amount of water content.

### Tertiary Butyl Alcohol Solution

One method of considerable merit, especially with certain flowers that refuse to respond to other techniques, was developed at the Florida Engineering and Industrial Experiment Station at Gainesville. Here researchers came up with eight different preserving solutions using tertiary butyl alchohol as the basic ingredient. Each of the eight basics includes additives that suit the needs of each color of flowers.

I have found the No. 1 solution to be the very best, if not the only way to preserve the whiteness of the lily of the valley, the shocking pink of the bleeding heart, and the contour and texture of the moss rose. The reason for this last success is that the moss itself contains and is coated with a sticky substance, to which any dehydrating material tends to cling very heavily; thus the cleaning job becomes impossible without ruining the delicate fibers. But these charming and distinctive fibers are not injured in this solution.

You can preserve the white of the lily of the valley, I found, by adding a few drops of blue flower dye to the solution in very much the same way that women add blueing to the white clothes in the Monday morning wash. This method has serious shortcomings, however. Because dehydrating time has been speeded up to from four to sixteen hours, the treated flowers are so fragile and brittle that it is almost impossible to place them in an arrangement without breaking them. I gather that the station's aim was to preserve the flowers for embedding in plastic. For this purpose the solution is ideal.

You may write the experiment station to request Bulletin Series No. 40 entitled "Preservation of the Color and Shape of Flowers," by Randolph C. Specht (Vol. 4, No. 12, December 1950). It costs $1.00.

CHAPTER IV

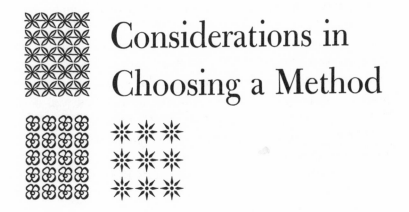

# Considerations in Choosing a Method

We have examined the methods you are most likely to use for preserving your flowers. In order to compare their merits, we must first determine our goals. All flowers have four characteristics that must be maintained if the preserved specimen is to resemble the original. Naturally, the medium that best preserves these characteristics is the one best suited for our purpose. So, let us consider them in order.

*1. Contour.* The first characteristic to be considered is the contour of the flower. It is the architectural structure with which we begin, and, like the art of building, it is governed by its own laws. The flower must be kept in its original shape and outline, and for this it needs support while it is drying. In order to have proper support for its wall structure, the flower needs to be under considerable pressure. This pressure must be distributed equally around, below, between, and on top of the petals to prevent the cell fibers from crumbling while the flower is being dehydrated. The drying material must not only have considerable weight, but it must also be fine enough to penetrate the innermost cavities of the flower and be able to flow freely through tiny openings without clogging them.

The commonly used cornmeal and borax preparation is somewhat weak in these requirements. Being rather irregular and adhesive, the grains tend to adhere to each other and fluff up;

‡‡ 27 ‡‡

thus, they sometimes fail to penetrate the innermost heart of the flower and must be "coaxed" in between narrow openings which sometimes distort the natural position of the petals, for some get too much of the mixture and others get too little. Because the mixture is fluffy, it cannot penetrate as readily as can a denser substance, such as sand. The uneven and inadequately distributed weight fails to support the walls of the flower very well during the dehydrating process and they may collapse. This accounts for the wrinkled appearance some flower petals have when taken out of this mixture.

On the other hand, oolitic sand meets these requirements if the proper technique of applying it is used. It weighs considerably more than the other desiccants and if distributed evenly leaves the flower with no other alternative than to emerge from the sand exactly as it went in. Furthermore, the more weight on top of the sand the better—the principle being somewhat the same as in the pressing of flowers, except that in this case, instead of being flat, the flower is preserved in its original three-dimensional perfection.

2. *Flexibility.* One of the chief differences between plastic and preserved flowers is the flexibility of the latter and it is also one of their principal charms. Fresh flowers have a great deal of flexibility so that we should try to maintain it in the dried ones if they are to appear natural. Also, there is more of a tendency for petals to break when cleaning them if they are not able to "give" a little. The same danger is present in the arranging and in the moving of the arrangement. So it becomes evident that this is a characteristic to be maintained at all costs.

Crisp, stiff petals are caused by too rapid and too great heating, which can be produced by borax. Indeed, people who use this method are warned not to leave the flower covered longer than necessary for it may actually burn.

This appears to be true also of the marketed silica gel. The drying time has been speeded up to one week, or just about half the time required by most other media. Unlike borax and cornmeal, however, it does not leave a white, powdery coating on the flower which is almost impossible to remove. It does leave

Comparison of results obtained with three different media. Blossoms at left have been properly preserved in Great Salt Lake oolitic sand. Roses in center, preserved in silica gel, are almost as successful, but betray some pitting, show lack of proper support, reveal clinging dust. Roses on right, done in borax mixture, are least successful, mainly because desiccating medium did not give uniform support.

Carnation on left, buried in sand, retains shape of flower and is clean of residue. One on right retains good form but is dusted over with the residue from desiccant, silica gel.

more particles sticking to the flower than does sand. Thus it is more difficult to clean because there is danger of breaking the rigid petals when you brush them.

In oolitic sand there are no excess caustics and acids to burn your flower, so you may leave your bloom buried as long as you wish. I have proved this to be true on several occasions when I inadvertently left flowers buried in the sand one full year. When I uncovered them, I found that they were just as soft and pliable as though I had taken them out after the allotted two weeks.

Ideally, you should be able to fill and cover a flower without moving a petal. With skill and patience you can do this with sand. In addition, it flows freely—much like water seeking its own level—so that no extra coaxing is needed. But this is only half the work that must be done. After the flower emerges from the desiccant, an equally important job remains—the job of grooming it and placing it in the arrangement where it is to remain permanently. The success of this procedure depends a great deal upon the ability of a desiccant to preserve flexibility. When choosing your desiccant, be sure to keep this important feature in mind.

*3. Color.* The range of color possibilities in preserved flowers is endless and the life of the flower or the bouquet is its color. It should be an aim of every flower dryer to duplicate in the preserved material the exact hue and tint of the fresh specimen. With care, this can be done.

The tendency is for most deep-toned flowers to take on a muted hue when dried. It is a softness that is found in Oriental rugs in which plant dyes are used. It is said that these rugs never clash with any color scheme or form of decor. So it is with these flowers. You can combine all the colors of the spectrum in an arrangement and they will look as if they were designed especially for any room in which they may be placed. Of course this is not true of the pastels and whites. They remain true, at least to a greater degree. But by the use of dyes, colors can be augmented or receded as the decorating need demands. Here again your experience in handling many flowers and your acquaintance with their habits will help you to obtain just what you want.

Colors vary with the type of drying material used. Again, it is advisable to compare and select the medium that will most nearly preserve the true tint of the fresh flower. Silica gel seems to give slightly better results than the borax and cornmeal. Neither of them, however, produces as true a color as the oolitic or treated sand. The alkali which goes into the composition of Great Salt Lake sand is capable of neutralizing acids. This may have a great deal to do with the clarity with which it preserves colors, particularly blue, lavender and purple tones.

Pink dahlias turn darker in silica gel than in sand. The white oleander takes on a cream color in silica gel, whereas it emerges pure white from the sand. But then again some whites are tricky and sometimes a cream color emerges that should be white. Yellow and orange shades are never sure of themselves; all come from the sand with the same true color they had in the garden, but, given a few months to stand, they eventually fade. It seems that Mother Nature made the mistake of using an unreliable grade of coloring material when she painted the yellow and orange varieties. But it is the flower dryer's aim to make up for these deficiencies by reinforcing the original color so that it will remain. This gives us a wider range of possibilities because we then have the choice of leaving the flower as it grew in nature or embellishing it as we see fit.

*4. Texture.* Here is where the ultimate test of medium and technique takes place. A woman with beautiful features and hair can have her looks ruined by a pockmarked complexion. And so it is with flowers. They may be perfect in form and color, but unless their petal surfaces are smooth and without blemish, they may as well be discarded.

It is obvious that this smoothness is produced by using a desiccant that will not produce these deformities. Those of irregular construction and contour must be ruled out. In addition to this, there must be no corrosive action on the petal surfaces. I demand that my flowers have sheen if it is present on the fresh flower. The weight of the drying material usually has something to do with this. In other words, a kind of ironing action takes place under the proper pressure and this, plus the fineness of the material, seems to do the trick.

A one-pound coffee can filled with oolitic sand weighs approximately four pounds. The same coffee can when filled with silica gel weighs around one pound, and about two pounds when filled with the borax and cornmeal preparation. Furthermore, the sand is able to penetrate into hidden cavities and crevices in the flower structure. Thus it can support the petals to their very tip ends, uniformly and evenly. Breakage in cell structure is minimized.

Examine the enlarged reproductions of the three different types of desiccants discussed in the previous chapter and study the texture of the sample flowers as they emerged from the various drying agents.

White oleander on left, preserved in sand, is clean and glossy. One on right, preserved in silica gel, is pitted, shows breakdown at edges.

# CHAPTER V

# The Sand Method: Preparation

The importance of preparation and care of the sand in flower preservation cannot be emphasized too strongly. A well-done job demands good tools. Merely collecting the sand is not enough. The raw sand of Great Salt Lake (or any other sand, for that matter) must be thoroughly prepared for its use as a drying agent.

### Washing the Sand

The sand used to dry flowers must be immaculately clean. I have known any number of friends to immerse a flower in raw sand —sometimes it came from a lake, a sand and gravel pit, or the backyard. They insisted that it was clean enough. The result was always the same—a complete failure. Any prospective flower dryer should mark well right from the start that any sand used in flower preserving must be washed and washed. The so-called "washed sand" that children's sandboxes are filled with is not what I call washed sand. Neither is the bagged material obtainable from the sand and gravel pits, which they insist is of clean quality.

Of course the instructions for cleaning sand are not applicable if you purchase Great Salt Lake sand in bagged quantities. The label rightly states that it has been washed and sifted and no further work on it is necessary. However, sand obtained from any other source MUST be thoroughly cleaned, even before you give it the special treatment that I mentioned earlier. It is well to know the proper method of washing sand in any event because you will eventually want to reclean your old sand, even if it is oolitic or synthetic oolitic.

Fill a bucket three-quarters full of sand. This will leave sufficient working room in the top quarter of the bucket so that the sand will not spill over the edges and clog the drain. Fill the bucket to the top with comfortably warm water. Stir and pull up the sand until it is thoroughly wet all through. At this point you will notice a considerable lowering of the water level for the sand absorbs the water very quickly. It may become necessary to add more water in order to complete the process.

Any foreign material present in the sand, such as twigs or leaves, will promptly come to the top and float on the water. If you do not have a garbage disposal unit, pour off this debris into a coarse sieve or colander; do not allow it to be washed down the drain. Tip the bucket carefully to one side so that the excess water drains off. Fill it again with warm water to about two inches above the sand. Add one tablespoon of detergent, soap powder or whatever washing agent you have on hand. Once again, lift, stir and turn the sand over and over until you are sure that every grain has received a thorough sudsing. This washing and rinsing process is best accomplished if you will concentrate on the sand at the bottom of the container. If the bottom layer is kept in agitation you may be sure the top will be also.

Work rather rapidly to keep the sand in constant motion so that it does not settle in a mass. Next, pour off the excess suds; one sudsing is all that is necessary. Now start the rinsing process. Fill the bucket again to the previous level and proceed with the clear water just as you did with the suds, lifting and turning the contents as before. Of course the number of rinsings will depend on how dirty the sand was in the first place.

To be sure that you have clean sand at the start, rinse too much rather than too little. The process should be repeated until the rinse water is clean and clear. Usually about fifteen minutes is sufficient cleaning time for average sand. This length of time is rather short, especially when you consider that you can use the sand year after year, without having to wash it again. The question has been asked, "How long can it be used without further washing?" The answer is that it can be used until it becomes obvious that it is dirty with debris: petals, bits of stems, leaves and, of course, dust. I have used mine sometimes twelve years without further washing. I do, however, sift it frequently to rid it of this extraneous material. But it is safe to say that it can be used many years without even doing this.

## Drying the Sand

Now comes the drying. There are three ways to do it:

1. The sand can be emptied into a large roasting pan and dried in a slow oven at about 250°. It will take four to five hours for it to dry. If this method is used, it is advisable to stir the sand occasionally. This hastens and insures uniform drying. This method is of especial value during wet weather, when drying outside is impossible.

2. My preference is for drying sand in the sun. The drying is faster and is not so messy, but it can be done only during warm, sunny days. Spread the sand thinly and evenly on a clean cloth on the lawn or terrace floor. Of course it must be in full sunlight. The drying time will depend on the time of the year. About two hours is necessary in midsummer, more during spring and fall.

3. The third method consists of laying the clean cloth on a basement floor. As with drying outdoors, spread the sand thinly and evenly. Drying can usually be accomplished overnight. This is perhaps the best method to use in the event you want to clean your sand during the winter months.

## Sifting the Sand

When it is perfectly dry, the sand must be sifted. This is necessary in order to remove all foreign particles which might harm petal surfaces. Coarse grains also are taken out so that what is left is pretty much of uniform size. Uniformity helps to equalize weight and bulk. Wire mesh, such as is found in the common tea strainer, is satisfactory for this sifting operation. A coarse mesh is to be avoided because it permits undesirable material to go through. Conversely, too fine a mesh holds back everything except the very finest grains and so creates waste. If you use a tea strainer, do not fill it completely full or unsifted sand will spill over the edges and contaminate the strained material.

Using a tea strainer is a rather slow and tedious process, so one of my students suggested a better one. She made a small wooden frame about six inches long and four inches wide. She then tacked a wire mesh of appropriate gauge to the bottom on all four sides of the frame. A narrow band of wood (plastic or cardboard would do) was tacked over the seams so that the weight of the sand could not cause the mesh to sag, thus permitting unwanted material to sift through the edges. This method is to be recommended because it is very much faster. In addition, it will be found to be a convenient gadget to use for grating chalk, which we will discuss later on.

I have found that the easiest way to sift a bucket of sand is to start with the following materials: an extra empty bucket, two empty tin containers such as one-pound coffee cans, a strainer and a small stick or spoon. Dip from the bucket of sand as much as the strainer will conveniently handle, having the strainer resting on an empty coffee can. You may shake the strainer, stir it with a small spoon, or both. When the strainer is empty of everything except the throw-away material, empty this refuse into the other empty coffee can before refilling the strainer with sand. When the first coffee can is full of strained sand, pour it into the empty bucket and start again. A pupil of mine reports that she was able to purchase a piece of nylon net of approximately the same mesh as the tea strainer. She fastened this over the top of a large container and sifted the sand through the net in a fraction of the time required by the tea strainer; a very good idea indeed.

## Treating the Sand

We have seen that sand possesses the weight and bulk necessary for holding the flower while it is being dried, but that ordinary sands have sharp ends and jagged edges which harm all flower surfaces. In order to overcome these handicaps and still make use of the sand process, I have evolved a method of treatment that can be used on any type of sand, anywhere, and if accurately applied will give about the same results as the Great Salt Lake variety. It is easy, takes little time and is inexpensive.

Measure out about fifteen pounds of dry, washed and sifted sand into a pan. Place sand in a medium hot oven until it is heated through. Remove the pan from the oven and add three tablespoons of melted paraffin wax. Stir with a large spoon until it is evenly distributed through the sand and until each grain is coated. This stirring process should take about five minutes. Let the sand cool, then add one tablespoon of bicarbonate of soda and one tablespoon of powdered or fine-mesh silica gel. Mix until the soda and gel are evenly distributed.

What actually happens is that the sharp points of the sand are encased in a hardened wax. Since the wax is water repellent, it becomes necessary to add a small amount of silica gel to absorb the moisture escaping from the flower. In other words, the moisture travels by capillary action around and through the sand, then is caught up and held while the drying takes place. Bicarbonate of soda makes the sand alkaline, like sand found near Great Salt Lake. Alkalinity contributes to the preservation of true color. In addition, treated sand acts as a polishing agent and the flower emerges from it with a beautiful sheen.

One word of admonition is in order before you do your mixing. Make sure your measurements are correct because too much paraffin will cause the sand to become matted and thus lose its ability to flow, so necessary to the proper covering of the flower. There are also dangers in too liberal a use of the other two additives.

The amount of sand that I have specified for treatment is arbitrary. If you are treating smaller amounts, divide the ingredients by one-third or, conversely, for larger amounts double the ingredients.

## Amount of Sand Needed

The amount of sand needed will depend on the kind of flowers and how many you wish to preserve. An ordinary one-pound coffee can, when full, contains about four pounds of sand and is sufficient for one rose, a hollyhock, or any flower of similar size. On the other hand, a spray of lilacs calls for about a bucketful.

The best way to begin flower preservation is to start with a limited amount of sand and then as your confidence and interest increase you can acquire more. Here is a simple rule of thumb. One container of sand will accommodate one flower (or spray) every two weeks during the blooming season. So, from one coffee can of sand can come twelve flowers from May to October. This, of course, does not include foliage which has to be treated in the same way. It should be noted that any flower dryer is going to have a number of experimental failures.

My estimate is that about fifty pounds would be sufficient for the needs of the average dryer. An even smaller amount can give a surprising collection of flowers, and it should be remembered that a little sand will go a long way.

I store my sand supply in large cardboard boxes whose seams and corners have been sealed with gummed paper to prevent leakage. One such carton should be sufficient for the average sand collection. I call it the supply box. But you should also have another such repository to hold your unwashed and untreated sand. Both should be conveniently placed and easily accessible so that you can add or take from them according to your needs. I keep an empty coffee can and bucket near each one.

# CHAPTER VI

# Containers

In the preceding chapter we readied the sand for use. Now comes the problem of what to put it in while you are preserving specimens.

When you take up the art of flower preserving, you will find that as success grows and imagination expands, you will not hesitate to use almost anything for a container. My husband, who was very fond of soup, complained one day that it had not been included in our menu for some time. Blushingly, I had to confess that all our soup bowls were in the basement, full of sand and marigolds, and that we would probably have to forgo soup during the blooming season. "I'm surprised," he remarked sarcastically, "that you haven't resorted to our gold-encrusted glassware."

What an idea! I had not thought of it. The very next day all of our gold-encrusted cocktail glasses disappeared into the basement. They were just right for some particular roses that I had been worrying about. All of which proves that almost anything can serve as a container for preserving flowers. However, there are some common, tried-and-true containers that you will find every bit as good as Wedgwood soup bowls or crystal tumblers. Also, you should know some of the standard rules for using them and for improvising your own with cardboard and gummed paper tape.

## One Flower to a Container

First of all, it is wise to allow only one flower to a container, unless otherwise indicated in the chapter entitled "Encyclopedia of Flowers and Their Special Treatment." There are some differences of opinion regarding this and some commercial flower dryers use boxes in which a great number of flowers are done at one time. However, getting one flower into and out of the sand without injury will probably demand just about all of the dexterity and attention that you can muster.

Anything will do that will hold sand and is of proper size to accommodate one flower with at least one extra inch of space above and around the bloom. At the very least, you will want to preserve the flower head, with just enough of the stem left for easy handling. Usually about an inch is enough.

### Types of Containers

The old-style squat one-pound coffee cans are ideal for most average-sized flowers such as roses, marigolds, daisies, and so forth. Tall fruit juice cans and the newer two-pound coffee cans are perfect for slightly longer sprays. Bowls, ice cream or milk cartons, in fact almost any kind of container can be utilized if it is leakproof and of sufficient size so that the flower is not crowded. On the other hand, long stalks of delphinium must have an unusually long box. Large sprays of lilacs require a carton cut to fit the spray.

### Making Containers

Making containers is not difficult. All one needs is a cardboard carton, scissors, a sharp knife, and a spool of gummed paper tape. After you have estimated the size of the flower to be preserved, cut the sides, ends, and bottom of the box from the carton. Then secure the sides and ends with the gummed paper to form an oblong or a square. The bottom is then taped on. It is necessary to put a strip of gummed paper on both the inside and outside of each seam. This gives added strength, for some boxes, when filled with sand, weigh from twenty-five to thirty-five pounds. Also, make certain that the four corners are well sealed; otherwise the sand will sift out. Like the sand, these boxes become a permanent acquisition and will last for years. If they are made of different sizes they can be stacked inside each other for storing. (See work pictures for the method of making containers.)

Containers may be made out of cardboard and gummed paper tape.

After the cardboard is cut, join the ends and sides with tape. Seams should be reinforced on inside.

Bottom is attached after the ends and sides are joined. Seal corners well to avoid leaks.

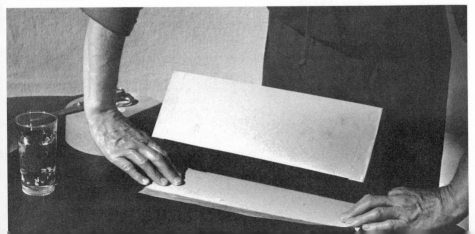

Almost any container is suitable for preserving flowers. If you use sand, the container should be sturdy.

### The "Mother Box"

The most important container of all and the one that will be in constant use is known as the "mother box." It is in this receptacle that you will do all of the covering and uncovering of your flowers, in and out of their individual containers. By so doing you will prevent messy scattering of your sand and also make instantly available an adequate supply of sand as you perform your tasks. In my classes, I provide each of my pupils with a mother box made of a cardboard carton approximately two feet long by one and one-half feet wide (such as you would find at the corner grocery store). They are too deep for easy access, so I cut down all four sides, leaving about six or eight inches all the way around. All of the seams and corners must be sealed with gummed paper to make them leakproof. Plastic or metal containers of similar proportions could also be used. My own mother box is a discarded baby bathtub.

It is well to make beforehand containers of various sizes from six to twelve inches square, depending on the sizes of the flowers you contemplate preserving. A tour of your garden, with flower sizes in mind, will confirm this and I cannot think of a more frustrating experience than to cut or be given a collection of beautiful flowers and find that you do not have enough containers to accommodate them. Be prepared for all contingencies. Remember that they can be used for many years if properly made, and you may bless the occasion, next year or in years to come, if you have them ready.

## *Collars*

Occasionally you may have a flower or spray that you wish to preserve and suddenly realize that you have no container tall enough to handle it. Whenever this occurs, select as deep a container as you can find. Cover as much of the flower as you can by filling the container to the top. To cover the part of the flower which is still exposed, cut a long strip of thin cardboard, shape it into a collar, and insert it into the sand around the flower as close to the inside edge of the container as possible. It should be long enough so that the ends can overlap. What you have done is simply to build up a continuation of the wall of the container so that the rest of the flower can be covered. The width of the strip of cardboard should be determined by the remaining height of the partially covered flower. For example, if you have three inches of uncovered flower remaining, your cardboard strip should be at least five inches wide. When inserted in the sand, this will take care of the flower's needs and give enough space for an extra inch of sand on top of the buried specimen.

Still another way to add an extension is to cut a portion from a cardboard milk carton, place it on top of the filled container, and then continue covering the flower. (See illustration on page 70)

A convenient way to store these collars is to press them flat in bunches of similar size and put an elastic band around them. Thus many can be stored in a large container without cluttering up your valuable workroom space.

I prefer a slightly different type of container for processing foliage. Since many pieces of foliage may be buried in the sand at one time, you must have room to accommodate the various types and also a portion of their original stems, so you will need a somewhat larger container than for flowers. This is particularly true with the fern and spray varieties such as maidenhair fern, mock orange, and Rosa hugonis. You may even wish to curve some of these stems, which also takes space. So make some containers that are long and wide but not too deep (keep in mind the cumbersome weight of each), in order to properly accommodate these specimens. You will be glad you did.

Another reason for having plenty of containers on hand is that when your flowers are removed from the sand, they are put on temporary stems which should be placed upright on a container of sand or soil for storage until they are used in an arrangement. (You may use unwashed sand for this so as not to waste your prepared sand.) Thus a great many flowers on stems of various lengths can be stored in one container, the only condition being that they do not touch one another.

This is a safe and convenient way to store them for the following reasons: (1) Flowers that emerge from the sand must never be laid down on a table or hard surface. By so doing, you may dislodge their petals and over a period of time they will become flattened and distorted. (2) Standing upright, they are safe and a casual glance at them from time to time in this close assembly will keep you informed as to their condition.

It is more convenient to place only one variety in a container, rather than several, because in this way you can readily determine how many of this particular variety you have on hand for use. There is no guesswork involved. The containers can be set, side by side, on shelves or tables with economy of space, which is of constant concern to the enthusiastic flower dryer.

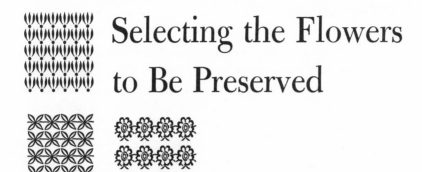 # Selecting the Flowers to Be Preserved

Probably the question most often asked by students is: "What flowers do I start with?" This question is more easily answered in the classroom than in a book because classroom students are required to start only with the simplest forms.

The principles and procedures for covering a single and double form may be the same, yet the psychological effects on the beginner are not the same. Until you get over that "all thumbs" feeling, you will do well to select single flowers for your first trials. By single flowers, I mean those with a single or semi-double row of petals, for example, single roses such as Elsie Poulsen and Rosa hugonis. The list of single flowers is long, with many new varieties coming on the market each year. It includes the single daisy, cosmos, hollyhock, Canterbury bell, clematis, tulip, and so forth. Therefore, the beginner should never be in want of material. Once you are successful with these, your growing confidence will indicate that you are ready to tackle the more complicated forms.

Doubles come next. These include the tea rose, double hollyhock, African marigold, peony, carnation, and so on. All are done in exactly the same way as the singles but require more skill and confidence.

After you have succeeded with the single and double flowers, you may wish to attempt to preserve sprays—lilacs, delphiniums, larkspur, fruit blossoms, bridal wreath—stems having multiple florets.

Most flowers can, with proper care, be successfully preserved, although some will generally do better than others. The "untouchables" are few; a list of these wayward creatures will be found in the section, "Encyclopedia of Flowers and Their Special Treatment." It grieves me to brand them as "lost souls," and I have not given up hope of some day bringing them under control. As a matter of fact, many have been reclaimed since the appearance of my first book. With the help of the moisture-proofing spray that is now available, quite a few can be dried successfully and will not flop, as they formerly did. Notable among these are the gladiolus, pansy, daffodil, rose of Sharon, campanula, crocus, day lily, evening primrose, and tradescantia.

There are some stubborn ones yet to be conquered. The lily of the valley is one of these. I have tried everything I ever heard of or know about and I still cannot preserve a lily of the valley that meets with my approval. The form preserves beautifully but, for some reason, it is one of those unpredictable whites that turn a parchment color when dried. The intrinsic beauty of this flower is its cool whiteness and nothing offends the name "preserved flowers" as much as a flower that should be white, but turns out tan. If nothing else does, this brands it as a "dried flower." I have hopes that this flower when dried and given a coating of Flower Sculpture Formula will regain its waxy white color and I intend to try it out next summer.

Then there is the portulaca—one of my favorite flowers. When I first started preserving flowers, I had visions of a bouquet of these with their satiny surfaces and jewel-like tones forever gracing my home. My fond hopes were soon shattered. They are so delicate in texture and the sand clings to them in such quantities that it is not only impossible to clean them without breaking the soft tissues, but they flop miserably as soon as they are removed from the sand. To dye them would be unthinkable because this would rob them of their most outstanding beauty—their jewel-like sheen. (Since writing this, I have discovered that a thorough dusting of the flower with baby talcum powder before it is put in the sand will prevent the sand from adhering to it. In fact, there is no cleaning necessary at all. Hurrah! Another lost sheep brought into the fold!)

The German iris is another stubborn flower. Probably its most outstanding beauty is the crystal-like texture of its delicate petals. Have you ever looked into the heart of a light blue iris? Do this sometime and imagine yourself living in that fragrant, crystal-blue dome. It is one of my favorite fancies. Yet, when I attempt to preserve the iris, the petals become transparent, like glass. Indeed it looks like a glass flower, and who wants that? Perhaps someone else will find a way to conquer this flower. I do hope so.

Even though we regret losing any one of nature's lovely children, there are still more than enough beautiful flowers left to preserve that will behave like angels and there are enough varieties to satisfy even the most discriminating tastes.

## Planning the Schedule

At this point it might be useful to pause and take a new look at your gardening plans. Unless you have some help, you may find yourself crowded for time if you plan to divide your spare hours between gardening and flower preserving. I offer this suggestion: plant more kinds, but fewer of each plant. Most amateur gardeners plant too much. They become overwhelmed with visionary beauty when they look through the spring seed catalogues and usually order more than they have time or room to plant. After you get started in flower preservation, you will *really* take a long look at your garden, with many changes in view. From the flower preserver's standpoint, you will concentrate on those plants which you wish to dry. They will be beautiful additions or you would not want to preserve them. So your garden will not suffer in appearance as a result of it. You will naturally want to have on hand the most perfect specimens you can get, so the accent will be on quality rather than on quantity. The wealth of drying material that can be had from one single, well-grown plant is amazing.

You must forgo some of your old habits and also develop some new ones. There must be no overhead watering. This invariably leaves the flower with water and pollen stains and breaks down the structure of the entire plant. So you will irrigate—the thing you should have done in the first place—for the good of your flowerbeds. The urgency of insect and mildew control will take on a new importance. Proper weeding, feeding and cultivation must be done if you are to produce blooms for preserving. In other words, you will become a more efficient and capable gardener when you take up the art of flower preservation, and your garden will take on a new look of beauty and well-cared-for maintenance.

I am experimenting with "pot gardening," the method used so successfully in India. The basic principle is to allow one annual to each pot. The pot is sterilized and filled with properly prepared soil best suited to the plant's particular needs. Thus, by rotating the placing of the pot, you can control sunshine and shade. Watering, insect control and feeding are made easier. If you have a sunny window or conservatory, the plant, pot and all, can be moved indoors when winter approaches so that you will have many blooms for winter drying.

I once had a pot of Maytime petunias that lived through three years of continuous bloom. Cutting the plant down periodically always stimulated new growth and I was continually amazed by the number of flowers that I had from this well-grown and cared-for plant.

## *Which Flowers Hold Their Color Best*

Stability of color in a preserved flower depends to a great extent upon the color as well as the variety of the flower; that is, some colors, regardless of the flower, last longer than others. The reds, pinks, blues, purples and lavenders hold their color very well. There may be a marked change in some of them after they are dried, but once stabilization takes place in the drying process, the color remains as long as the flower lasts. Reds and purples grow darker. Most lavenders take on a bluish tinge. Pinks and blues remain true but some of them have a tendency to fade a bit after a period of time. Darker shades do not fade; they remain the same year after year.

With flowers in the red category, it depends on just what tone of red you want to achieve. Most reds turn darker in the sand. The student may choose a blood-red rose, submerge it in the sand and expect it to come out with the same luscious tone it had when it grew on the bush. This is never the case. When working with reds, it is generally best to select a flower lighter in color than the color you wish to see in the finished product. An orange-red will usually produce a true red. An example of this is the Floradora, a Floribunda rose of salmon red on the bush but which comes from the desiccant a true red. The Tropicana is a typical example of a hybrid tea rose which does the same thing. Also, if you choose a flower with a lighter shade than you really want, you can always dye it the proper shade before you submerge it in the sand.

As I said in the beginning, much depends on the flower. For example, the red peony comes from the desiccant with exactly the same coloring that it had when it was fresh and it NEVER fades.

I have found the following red flowers to be satisfactory when dried: rose, zinnia, stock, scarlet sage, peony, poinsettia, ocotillo, hollyhock, fuschia, carnation, dahlia, crape myrtle, cockscomb, cactus, bougainvillea, azalea, aster and anemone. There are others and the adventurous student will find them.

I suspect there are probably more pink flowers in cultivation than any other color. It seems that everybody loves them. I cannot offhand think of any other color that dries more beautifully. The entire range of hues from the flesh tints through the medium and strong pinks to the dark rose tones are both useful and beautiful. I submit a partial list of pink flowers that I preserve every year and which I can heartily recommend to the reader: ALL pink roses, larkspur, water lily, carnation, peony, zinnia, azalea, fruit blossoms, hydrangea, painted daisy, chrysanthemum, hollyhock, aster, gladiolus, stock, dahlia, cosmos, snapdragon, candytuft, pink bachelor's button, cyclamen and cactus. Some of these flowers can be reinforced in color before preserving. Others cannot. Let the surface texture of the flower be your guide; still others can be shaded a bit, such as the slight tinting of the heart of a rose with a bit of darker chalk. This is where the artistry of the flower preserver asserts itself.

A perfectly preserved blue flower always creates a sensation. Perhaps it is because there is not a very impressive list of true blue flowers in general cultivation. Those that are considered worthy of today's gardens are worth preserving in every instance. Lavenders and purples are closely allied to them; in fact, most lavender flowers take on a blue tone when dried. It is for this reason that I shall group them together in listing the best varieties for preservation. What can surpass the blue delphinium? It emerges from the desiccant exactly as it went in and stays that way! Then there is the bachelor's button, scabiosa, forget-me-not, lobelia, globe thistle, pentstemon, blue pansy, tradescantia, blue rose of Sharon, blue lace flower, love-in-a-mist, blue hydrangea, gentian and others. With purples and lavenders, you must include lilac, larkspur, clematis, violet, purple and lavender zinnia, tulip, stock, sweet pea (pink ones turn lavender), phlox, lythrum (pink turns lavender), hollyhock, dahlia, aster and false dragonhead.

The yellow and orange flower world would include: ALL marigolds, yellow roses, acacia, basket-of-gold, buttercup, cactus, coreopsis, daffodil, dahlia, lemon lily, doronicum, evening primrose, gloriosa daisy, hollyhock, Oregon grape and tulip. It will be noted that the same flowers are included in more than one color category. This is because the flower itself dries equally well, regardless of color.

Practically all green plant tissue owes its color to chlorophyl pigmentation. As far as I know there is no way to prevent the eventual disappearance of this color in the preserved specimen. Greens emerge fresh and true in color but eventually, like yellows, begin to fade. Dyeing the greens before you preserve the plants will double their life span. But a treatment that is more lasting even than this and one that I have adopted is to spray the foliage after it is dried. Thus its fresh green look will last as long as the foliage itself endures. This will be discussed in detail in a later chapter.

Each white flower seems to follow its own laws. Certain of the near-white and apparently-white flowers contain tannin compounds together with substances which are more or less colorless in the natural state but are capable of developing color when oxidized. I once buried a snow-white camellia and it came out of the desiccant the same white, but after several weeks it turned tan, then became pink, which it remained. Thus it is that

Preserved hybrid lily treated with flower sculpture formula.

Peace Rose

Preserved Japanese tree peony treated with flower sculpture formula.

Zinnias

Arrangement of marigolds, dock,
and brown yarrow in a Japanese
container.

Single tree peonies, powder-puff hollyhocks, butterfly bush, roses, stocks, hydrangeas, and spiraea arranged in Venetian glass. Foliage is glycerinized myrtle and golden rain.

Hogarth line arrangement in autumn colors: zinnias, gladioli, yarrow, roses, butterfly bush, dahlias, powder-puff hollyhocks, goldenrod, and seedpods from the golden rain tree. Foliage is glycerinized camellia leaves.

Forget-Me-Not

Globe Mallow

Clover with Crested Wheat

Dogtooth Violet

Hollyhock with Pennycress

Fringed Gentian with Mustard Hedge

Big Leaf Balsam

Common Phlox

Indian Paintbrush with Indian
Rice Grass

Silver candelabra decorated with red roses; red roses arranged in a crescent design in a silver bowl.

Arrangement of yellow flowers: roses, powder-puff hollyhocks, dahlias, and spiraea.

All white arrangement of water lilies, Marconi daisies, spiraea, mock orange, roses, and baby's breath.

some whites are so unpredictable. On the other hand, certain true-white flowers seem devoid of pigmentation and show little or no tendency to discolor after drying. Since the whiteness is due to a diffused reflection from nearly transparent cell walls, these flowers become nearly translucent, almost transparent, after the natural juices are withdrawn. This happens to the white iris, sego lily, and others. A light brushing with soft, high-grade white powdered chalk will restore the opaque look.

Among the white flowers that I have found to be most satisfactory are: lilac, mock orange, daisy, larkspur, Canterbury bell, peony, fruit blossoms, cosmos, water lily, tulip, snowball, snowdrop, hydrangea, Queen Anne's lace, rose, petunia, hollyhock, oleander, narcissus, azalea, calla lily, columbine, bridal wreath and aster. It adds up to an imposing enough list to satisfy most white-flower lovers.

## *When to Cut Flowers for Preserving*

Probably the main reason for failures in flower drying is imprudent and untimely cutting. A flower comes out of the drying material exactly as it goes in. A withered living flower comes out a withered dry one. Thus it becomes obvious that a flower must not be picked except at the height of its beauty and must be processed before that perfection begins to fade. This does not necessarily mean that all flowers must be in full bloom when they are picked. Any stage of bloom you wish is all right provided the flower is crisply fresh.

Do not cut flowers during the heat of the day. Early morning or late evening is better. Do not cut too many at one time. Even with small flowers, two or three at a time is enough, and even then, put their stems in water immediately after cutting to keep them fresh until you can get them into the sand.

I once had a famous rosarian tell me the proper way to keep roses. As soon as they are cut, put the stems in water as hot as your hand can endure. Then let them cool in the same water. They will last for days, allowing you to do anything you want with them. One of my pupils contributed another flower-keeping solution: to a quart of cold water, add three tablespoons of sugar, one-third teaspoon of Clorox and one-third teaspoon of powdered alum. Pound the stem ends lightly and put them into this solution. As the water evaporates, add more of the same solution, not just plain water. I have found this formula most helpful to take along when collecting wild flowers.

Do not cut more than one flower of the larger varieties such as delphinium, peony, or lilac. It may take longer than you think to process and your second cut flower might lose its crispness before you are ready for it.

Do not cut flowers that are wet. After a rain or a watering, leave the flower in the garden until it has dried out. It has a better chance of retaining its freshness on the bush while it dries than in the house. Make sure your flower is thoroughly dry before processing. One drop of water hidden somewhere in the heart of the flower will cause it to turn brown. In spite of our utmost care, there are occasions when a flower such as the water lily must be cut, even when wet. It is seldom that a water lily can be found free from moisture or aphides, and the aphides must be washed off before the lily can go into the drying material. In such cases, you must have ready small camel's hair paintbrushes of varying sizes. I buy them by the dozen. Start wiping off the moisture, center and stamens first, then progressing to the petals. You must do these one at a time and when you have completed the face of the flower, do the back of the petals. When one brush becomes saturated with water, discard it for a dry one and continue wiping. Go back over the heart of the flower and deep down where the petals are joined to the calyx. All must be thoroughly dried before the flower withers.

Brush-drying may be used in emergencies when the flower dryer is presented with a gift of blooms from some well-meaning friend who cut them while they were wet or even sprinkled them generously with water to keep them fresh. Flowers purchased from a nursery or florist often arrive in this "sprinkled" state and should be thoroughly brushed before processing. It would also be advisable to give them the "sure-fire" test for hidden moisture. (See the chapter, "Dyeing Preserved Flowers.")

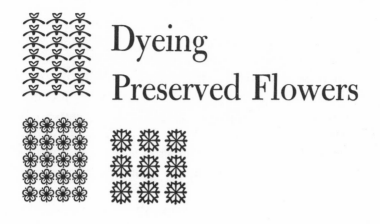

# CHAPTER VIII

# Dyeing
# Preserved Flowers

To many people, the idea of dyeing flowers will seem repugnant. After all, how can one improve on nature? And isn't the very purpose of flower preservation to keep flowers as lifelike as possible? Most of us will readily agree that to dye flowers indiscriminately is to deface them, but there are times when dyeing is necessary. Sometimes a dried flower will lose its color before we can place it in an arrangement. This is no fault of ours nor of the method we have used to preserve it. The worst offenders, and I might even say the only ones, belong to the yellow and orange classifications. The yellows emerge from the sand clear and true, but, alas, after a few months of exposure, begin to show streaks of white. Orange-colored flowers seem to last a few months longer but after about a year these, too, begin to fade. So, we restore it to its original color before proceeding with the arrangement.

Then there are occasions that demand a specific color combination rarely seen in nature. For example, I have had many requests for turquoise-colored flowers. No other color would do. A true blue or lavender blue screams louder than an eagle in a particular room. It must be turquoise. Now where on this earth is anyone going to find turquoise flowers? Yet the need must be answered if the customer is to be satisfied. What do I do in such cases? I simply give them flowers that have been tinted turquoise.

## Dyeing Preserved Flowers

There are times when texture as well as color changes occur in nature. Zinnias have a texture rough to the touch, yet a velvety appearance while in the garden. Before they reach full maturity of bloom, however, they often become scarred or water-marked because of wind, rain, or other natural causes. They may be perfect in form, yet carry such disfigurations. And, of course, all blemishes, as I mentioned earlier, become more prominent after a flower is dried. I find that a light brushing with a powdered chalk exactly the same color as the flower, will not only restore the velvety texture, but will also cover up any little imperfections and give the flower the same appearance it had before it was damaged.

There are also times when it is necessary to dust a stem, leaf, or flower, not for the purpose of stabilizing the color, but to keep the sand from adhering too thickly to its surfaces, making the leaf or flower particularly difficult to clean.

The petunia is one of the most flagrant examples of this dyeing for the purpose of easier cleaning. All flower growers, I am sure, are familiar with the sticky feeling of the stems and the undersurfaces of the petunia. A test can be made by submerging two flowers in the sand—one, just as it grew in the garden, and the other, one that has been brushed on its undersurface (never on its face), with properly colored chalk. An appropriate green should also be brushed on the stem and leaves. When they are dried and removed from the sand, it will be found that the chalked flower can be more easily cleaned than the unchalked one. Indeed, it is impossible to clean a petunia, without danger of breakage, unless it is chalked beforehand. (A discovery that I made since the writing of this chapter supersedes this chalk method, in my own estimation. The substitution of baby talcum powder for the chalk seems to make the cleaning easier. However, I include both methods in order to let the reader judge for herself which one she prefers.)

The blue of the bachelor's button is one of the finest in the flower kingdom. Yet it, too, will lose its vivid hue unless the color is fortified a bit. If you will observe a plant of bachelor's buttons in full bloom, you will notice that those that opened today or even a few days ago are clear and strong in color. Yet some others have faded to a lighter blue and others again have even turned white. It seems that it is one of the flowers that really gets old—white hair and all. The same performance takes place in the desiccant unless you prevent it. It took me four months one summer to overcome this difficulty. I found that by reinforcing the color and speeding up the drying process, the beautiful color of the bachelor's buttons could be preserved and that they would last virtually forever. This summer I used some in an arrangement that were eleven years old, along with some others that I preserved this year. I could not see any difference between them.

The process that I finally adopted for use on them was to mix a liberal amount of powdered chalk (dark blue, a bit of lavender and a dash of green) with about one quart of sand. I then covered the bottom of a shallow pan with the mixture and placed the flower heads, face up, on this bed, with enough space between each flower for easy covering. I put the pan containing the covered flowers in a very slow oven for about two hours. When cool I uncovered them. This method proved to be so successful that I never again had a faded bachelor's button. There are further directions regarding the preparation of the flowers that will be given in detail in the "Encyclopedia of Flowers and Their Special Treatment."

I have come to believe that preserved plant collections for museums and historical societies should have their colors reinforced before they are presented as permanent acquisitions. I realize that I may be facing a good deal of criticism in making such a statement. On the other hand, this is preferable to the alternative of having the preserved material fade in color after a number of years. It is a tremendous undertaking to collect, preserve and arrange even a modest representation of plant material; it requires experience and skill to execute it properly. The material should be protected against any contingency, such as moisture, exposure to strong light, and so forth. Therefore, it should be reinforced for color permanence and sprayed for maintenance of contour; if this is expertly and carefully done, the collection can become a truly permanent and valuable acquisition.

## Dyeing Preserved Flowers

In these cases dyeing is legitimate. Yet most of us who dry flowers love them the way they are; we avoid dyeing them except when we have very good reasons.

*Never exhibit dyed flower in shows.* It goes without saying that preserved flowers to be used in exhibits or for scientific study in classrooms should never have their colors or textures touched up. In shows their values are judged by their natural merits and classroom study is based on the same principle. Flowers for either use are not designed for keeping. Tinting should be confined to commercial and home use, with the possible exception of permanent displays. Be honest even then; do not try to hide the fact that a particular flower has been dyed.

## Methods of Dyeing Flowers

There are two accepted methods of dyeing flowers: liquid dye, which is available or can be ordered through most florist shops and powdered chalk, which you can buy in sticks at a school supply store and prepare yourself. I have practically discontinued the use of liquid dye for the following reasons: It is offered for sale in quart jars only and is very expensive. The average flower dryer cannot possibly use this amount of dye during a season; the dye will deteriorate after a short time, lose its strength, and will not give the intensity of color desired. Then, too, I have found that the flower loses some of its freshness before the dye becomes dry enough to submerge the flower in sand. It often drips in excess on the lower petals of a fully double flower, thus leaving a spotted look.

In spite of these drawbacks, there are some flowers that respond better to the liquid dye than to any other. These are to be found among those that do not need to be buried in sand but belong to the hang and dry classification. They include such flowers as chive, yarrow, baby's breath, goldenrod, everlastings, and so forth.

For the benefit of those readers who would still like to try it for themselves, here are the directions: Dip the flower in the dye bath and let the excess dye drip back into the container. A slight shaking of the flower over the container will help this along.

Now place the flower stem in a container of cold water to keep the flower fresh and crisp while the liquid is drying on it. Remember, the flower must be completely dry before it is put into the sand. If there is any doubt in your mind, it would be well to give it the "sure-fire" test for unseen, hidden moisture described later in this chapter before submerging your flower.

White flowers may be dyed any color. Pastels may be made darker or even slightly changed in hue by dipping them in a color that differs from their natural tone. Do not try to make a dark flower lighter; it cannot be done.

## The Chalk Method

The chalk method, as mentioned, is the preferred method of dyeing flowers. Unfortunately, chalk is not available in powdered form, so you will be forced to buy the sticks and grate your own. Go to a store that carries school supplies and select what you think you may need. Insist upon getting the finest grade of chalk available, which is a soft chalk. Do NOT buy a hard chalk, because you cannot grate it. I buy a brand called "Ambrite," which comes in boxes of solid or mixed colors. It is manufactured by the American Crayon Company, Sandusky, Ohio. There are twelve sticks to a box. The white is sold separately and comes in large boxes (one gross). The brand name is Waltham, so ask for the soft grade used in school classrooms.

I have tried pounding it, rolling it, and grinding it only to end up with tired muscles and not very good results. The best way is to grate it. The simple, sand-sifting gadget described in Chapter V, "The Sand Method: Preparation," is ideal for this purpose, or you may place a piece of finely meshed screening over a large bowl or container and grate through that. I advise using a container that has a hard surface rather than a cardboard one because the chalk clings to the cardboard and is not easily removed and, of course, it cannot be used for anything else.

Grate each color separately and put each finished product in a separate large plastic bag. You will need more of the white than the colored because it is the base for all lighter tones. It is well to have as many different colors as are available because you will have to mix the colors to suit individual flower groups and you will soon discover that there are no pure colors in nature, but a mixture of colors, with one predominating tone. The chalk comes only in strong colors, but by using white chalk for a base and then gradually adding small amounts of strong colors, a lighter hue is obtained. For example, let us say that you need a pink. Pour out a quantity of powdered white chalk in a bowl and then add some red, a very little at a time, stirring constantly until it is thoroughly blended. If you desire a darker pink, add more red; if a lighter pink, add more white. This is the way to get all light colors—blue, lavender, or whatever.

Sometimes you may need a color not found in nature, such as turquoise. This is produced by starting with the usual white base, then adding blue, a small amount of light green, and often a dash of yellow. Experiment and play around with these combinations until you get the exact shade that you desire. If you want a muted rose, add a dash of lavender and gray to the rose mixture. A bit of yellow and orange will produce coral. Rarely ever do you use a straight color. A slight sample on the flower petal will tell you this. So study your flower and endeavor to combine the colors that will be indiscernible when applied to it.

Yellows rarely need diluting with white unless you wish to make a cream color. In this event, a very little yellow and a dash of brown added to the white base will usually suffice. There are times when a green-yellow or chartreuse color is needed. In this case, omit the white and start with a yellow base. Add as much light green as is needed to produce the exact shade. White, it must be remembered, is a lightening agent while gray and brown produce muted colorings.

As each shade that meets with your satisfaction is produced, empty the contents into a separate plastic bag, close it with a rubber band and see that it is conveniently placed for immediate use. I stress this word "immediate" because the flower must be dyed while it is still fresh; if it is to remain so until it is covered with the sand, there will not be time enough after it is cut to start mixing your chalk, nor even to start looking around for the right bag of color. So have your correct materials on hand.

## The Sure-Fire Moisture Test

The flower must be perfectly dry before powdered chalk can be applied. Often a flower looks dry but may still contain hidden drops of moisture in its center. This is particularly true of double flowers. There is a "sure-fire" test that can be given the flower in order to determine if this is the case. Hold the flower upright with the left hand; with the right hand sprinkle sand lavishly over the whole thing, making sure a liberal amount reaches the heart of the flower. Now tip the flower face downward and tap the stem briskly with a pencil or stick. If any particles of sand still cling to the flower, it is wet and the sand has captured the moisture and held it there. Having once discovered the moisture by this test, you must continue sprinkling over and through the flower. Again turn it upside down and again tap the stem smartly. Repeat the process until the flower comes through the last tapping clean and free from sand particles. It is now ready to be preserved. Caution: Do not allow damp sand to fall into your mother box, as it will contaminate the sand supply with moisture. Use a side container to catch it. It can then be dried for reuse.

The easiest and most commonly used method of dyeing flowers is to drop the flower in the plastic bag containing the powdered chalk, press the open end together and gently shake the flower around in the bag. This is very much like the procedure of flouring a chicken before cooking. Now pick up the flower by its stem. With its head pointed downward, tap the stem smartly with a pencil or stick. This will remove some of the excess but not all of it. Next, brush the petals with a camel's hair brush to loosen more of the chalk. Now tap again. Next, hold the flower over a container of sand (unwashed will do) and let handfuls of the unwashed sand flow over and through the petals. Do this several times, rotating the flower as you proceed. Now tap the stem again, letting the sand and chalk fall, this time into the container of unwashed sand. This should remove all of the remaining excess chalk from the flower, leaving only the stain, which is what we are striving for. If you are still unsure, go over the process again. Now the flower is ready to be covered. This method is used for flowers such as the double hollyhock, roses, marigold, in fact all flowers that do not have prominent stamens or centers. These must be handled in another way.

The second method is used for flowers that DO have yellow centers which would be ruined in appearance if the centers were to be dyed the same color as the rest of the flower. I refer to such flowers as water lilies, daisies, single roses, zinnias, etc. There can be no submerging for these.

The dye is brushed on the flower with a camel's hair brush, petal by petal until the entire flower has been covered. This includes the underside of the petals also. Since the accumulation of chalk is not as great on the flower as in the previous method, a light brushing with a clean brush should be sufficient to remove any excess. The brushing will improve the appearance of the flower because it helps to distribute the color more evenly.

The yellow centers must also be reinforced with the appropriate color of chalk and a very thin brush. Be very careful that you do not break the stamens and that you do not allow the yellow chalk to overlap on the colored petals. If this does accidentally happen, go over the petal lightly with more chalk of its own color.

When the flower is dried and taken from the sand, you may discover that there are some spots that remain undyed or you may be disappointed with the color of the dye you chose. They can be given another coat of chalk to remedy these errors. Before you do, however, spray the flower lightly with moisture-proofing spray and let it get completely dry. If the first coat of dye was applied with a brush, you may now go over the flower again, in the same way. If the flower is of the double variety and was dyed in the plastic bag, you must resort to a third way of dyeing.

After a flower has been dried, it must never again be submerged in the plastic bag. If you did, it would break it into pieces. The brush method would not be practical because of the multiplicity of petals and the time-consuming and difficult job of covering them. A better method is to hold the flower or spray over a sheet of plastic, then fill a tea strainer with the powdered chalk and shake the contents over the flower, rotating the flower as you proceed. Repeat the process several times. Gently tap the stem and follow with a gentle sand blasting.

There are flowers that should NEVER be dyed. I refer to the ones whose colors are stable and unchangeable such as the larkspur, delphinium, peony, and so forth. Then there are those whose petals resemble shining silk or satin. To touch up these beauties would rob them of their most attractive features. Examples would be the cactus, single peony, godetia or any other flower whose lustrous surface would be ruined by the application of dye.

These, then, are the principal methods of dyeing flowers. The process begins with the fresh flower, so see that your materials and tools are ready to use before you proceed to the treatment of the flower itself.

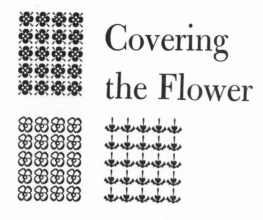

# CHAPTER IX

# Covering the Flower

Covering is the crux of flower preservation. This operation contributes most to success or failure. It requires the skill which can be acquired only through practice. Do not worry about an occasional failure. There are always some. But failures are soon forgotten when success finally comes, bringing the thrill of seeing a perfectly done flower. The acme of skill is to be able to cover a flower in its entirety without disturbing the natural position of a single petal or stamen. And you will be surprised how quickly you can achieve this.

Before proceeding, you must first make sure that all of your materials are ready to use and close at hand. You should take an inventory to make certain of this.

You have prepared the sand, which is stored in a large, conveniently placed container within easy reach of your working area. Your individual containers are ready; you have calculated their number and size requirements. Collars are cut and easily available. Your chalk has been powdered and the colors mixed to your satisfaction. Scissors, pins, paintbrushes, pliers, notched cardboard props, a fine sieve, a roll of wax paper, pencil and labels are all ready to be called into their proper use. Your flowers have not yet been cut, I hope, because you are not yet ready to process them. There still remains some preliminary work to do before you are ready to tackle the "real" thing.

## Covering the Flower

Place the mother box on a table low enough so that while you are seated before it, you will not have to lift your arms unnaturally in order to reach the box. Yet the table should not be so low that you are forced to stoop. A natural, relaxed position is important.

The directions and proportions for the mother box were given in Chapter VI, "Containers." It is to be hoped that it will remain in this permanent place that you have selected for it because all of the work from now on that has to do with the covering and uncovering of the flower will be done within this box.

The table should be placed under a strong artificial light. Daylight is good, provided you are never forced to do your work in the face of strong sunlight; this could be very annoying. I prefer the placement away from a direct light because daylight can vary according to the time of day and there will be times when you will want to work at night. Adequate artificial light never varies, night or day, and your eyes will soon become adjusted to this light, since it will always be of the same intensity.

You will need a pointed stick (an orange stick or discarded paintbrush—its use will be seen later on) and the particular container that you have selected for your flower.

Fill your mother box about half full of sand and try to keep it half full. There should be an empty bucket and a tin container nearby for this purpose because nothing is as annoying and time wasting as scraping around the box trying to collect a handful of sand.

## Hand Technique for Applying Desiccant

Each student, before she processes a flower, should first familiarize herself with the "feel" of the sand, or whatever medium she uses. Applying the sand to the flower is ALWAYS done with the hand, never with a spoon, sifter or anything else. It is impossible to control the flow of the sand any other way. With a little practice, you will see what I mean.

Grasp a small handful of sand. If too much is grasped, it will sift through your fingers. Hold your palm up and tip it sideways, letting the sand flow slowly and evenly through the opening where the little finger meets the palm. Stop the flow by raising

Sand for covering the flower is released from small opening of closed hand.

the palm upward to its original position. Starting and stopping can be controlled by a slight twist of the wrist. Next, with the palm tilted toward the side, practice controlling the volume of sand by tightening and relaxing the fingers. You will observe that the flow can be regulated at will, from a few grains to a stream. Do this several times. Now again grasp a handful of sand and with the palm tilted move your hand in a circle. You will note that the flow of sand thus may be made to resemble a jet stream, capable of moving instantly in any direction to any point.

To stop flow of sand, turn hand to palm-up position. Rate of flow can be controlled by tightening or releasing grip on sand.

## Covering the Flower

Never allow the sand to come from the opening between thumb and index finger because, here again, control will be lost, and you must be master of the situation at all times. A few minutes of practice at this before you attempt your first flower is not only advisable, but necessary. Very soon you will be using the right technique, very much as the typist strikes the right keys on the typewriter.

After practicing this technique until such time as you think you have acquired it and have it under control, you are ready to cut your flower. Bring it immediately into your working room and shear off the accompanying foliage. There will be times when you won't do this, but for the moment it must be a stripped specimen. You will have all you can do to concentrate on the treatment of the flower itself without worrying about accompanying foliage.

You have already made up your mind as to whether you wish to dye the flower or do it in its natural state. If you have decided to dye it, now is the time to do it. First make sure the flower is dry, then proceed according to the type of flower chosen and the method outlined in Chapter VIII, "Dyeing Preserved Flowers."

## Cutting the Stem

Because stems dry naturally, why waste effort, space, and sand on them? Besides, you may wish to attach the dried flower to a wire stem instead of to a natural one. For these reasons, only about an inch of stem is to be left on the flower before processing or just enough to assure easy handling.

If you wish to return the flower to its original stem after it is dried, insert a pin into the stem end of the flower. Aim for the center of the stem. Do it carefully and slowly. Embed the pin deeply enough so that the stem will hold it securely, then cut the pin off, leaving about one-half inch protruding. You should also insert a pin in the cut end of the parent stem while it is still fresh. (See Chapter XI, "How to Prepare Stems.") After the flower dries, its stem will be too hard to receive the pin. Therefore, if you develop the habit of putting a pin into the stems of most flowers you preserve, you will always be able to restore them to the parents or to some other stem at a later time. Choose only flowers that have stems sufficiently thick to hold the pin for this treatment—roses and fruit blossom clusters are particularly amenable to this procedure. Flowers whose stems are too thin and fragile to hold a pin will have to be taken care of in another way.

If you are processing fruit blossoms, cut off each cluster as close to the mother branch as possible, insert the pin and process the cluster. Before you proceed to the next cluster, you must insert a pin in the mother branch, at exactly the point from which the cluster was cut. You may also wish to restore the dried cluster to the branch at the same angle it had when it was fresh, so take note of this as you cut the cluster, and insert the pin in the branch at the same angle you wish the cluster to assume when finished. The reason for this is clear when you consider that in assembling the dried clusters, you must first withdraw the pin from the mother branch, and in doing so a hole is left into which the pin, holding the cluster, is placed. A bit of glue on the pin will hold it securely. Thus an entire branch of fruit blossoms may be preserved, exactly as they grew on the tree.

### Positioning the Flower

A flower may be buried in one of three positions—face up, face down, or horizontal. Over ninety percent, however, are processed face up. With many flowers, only one position is best, but with others the dryer may position the flower according to her personal preference. After a little experience, she will be able to tell at a glance which method the flower demands. As has been mentioned earlier, it is wise to allow only one flower to a container, in most cases. The techniques described in this chapter were developed for use with sand, but they may also be used with silica gel or borax and cornmeal as a desiccating agent.

### Face-Up Position

The container should be roomy enough to permit an inch of drying medium all around the flower—bottom, top, and sides.

Start by putting the one-inch layer of sand or other desiccant in the bottom of the container. The stem should be completely buried and the lowest row of petals should rest naturally and lightly on the sand. If one inch is not enough, add more. This cushion must be smooth and level before receiving the flower. If you gently shake the box, the sand will be its own leveler. No sort of scraper is needed.

Hold the flower gently by the calyx, or from the underside of the lower petals, with the stem pointed downward over the center of the sand bed. Pick up the pointed stick with your free hand and agitate the sand rapidly, but only at the exact spot where the flower stem is being inserted. The stem will then glide easily and quickly to the desired depth without damage to the petals, which will occur if the flower is forced in.

The face of the flower must be looking straight up at you. See to it that it is *straight*, not at an angle; the flower must be in its natural position as it is being covered. Otherwise, it is liable to become crippled in the drying agent. If it is deformed when it goes into the sand, it will be deformed when it comes out.

Now let a handful of sand flow along the inside edge and corners of the container as far away from the flower as possible. Build up the outer edge about one-half inch. Then gently tip the container once in each direction. The sand will flow toward the flower and even itself off. Repeat this operation until the

Covering flower takes two hands: right hand supplies sand, left straightens tangled petals with pointed stick.

lower petals are partially covered and anchored in place. You will now notice that the sand level is higher in the area surrounding the flower than it is in the center of the flower. Let a thin stream of sand flow gently from your hand over the stamens and through the petals. When the sand in the container is level again, the flower will be firmly anchored. The petals cannot push inward or outward, but must remain in place while you continue to cover them. Keep your hand close to the box at all times during the covering process. A common mistake that most beginners make is to hold their hand too high in the air, letting the sand fall where it will, thus losing control of the sand. Watch this very carefully. Develop the correct habits consciously, from the beginning, and then later they will become automatic.

After sand touches the center of the flower, do not tip the container again. From this point on, all that remains is to complete the covering. As you do so, make sure the sand is level at all times, in and through the flower, and to the edges and corners of the container. Alternately let a little sand flow outside and inside the flower until you have covered it completely and the box is full. Now tap the container gently on all four sides to fill in any possible air pockets. If the sand level lowers and bits of the petals emerge, add more sand. Label the box with the date and name of the flower and set it away in a warm place to dry. The drying time will depend on the type of flower being preserved. Two weeks is the average time for most flowers, but there are exceptions. (See Chapter XVIII, "Encyclopedia of Flowers and Their Special Treatment.")

Exceptions: The procedure that I have described is for the many flowers that are best preserved at maturity, but there are many times when it is desirable to preserve flowers at other stages of bloom. You may like the cup shape of the single rose, hollyhock or some other flower. Most people, I have observed, feel that a flower at this stage of bloom is more graceful and appealing than when its petals stand outright and stiff.

To preserve this contour, cover the flower as directed earlier, but keep the level of the sand slightly higher on the outside of the flower than on the inside as you proceed with the covering. Regulate the mount of sand according to the degree of cupping you wish to achieve. By the time you have reached the top of the flower, the pressure on the inside must equal that on the outside of the flower or the flower will collapse inwardly.

If you wish to preserve the graceful inverted cup of the Esther Read daisy or the drooping line of a double marigold, dahlia, carnation, etc., omit the one-inch cushion of sand on the bottom of the container and start with it empty. Let sand flow from your hand onto the exact center of the container bottom. Do this several times. You will observe that a smooth, even, volcano-shaped mound builds up. Insert the flower, stem straight down, through the tip of the sand volcano, so that the drooping petals rest on its sloping sides. The mound provides a perfect support for maintaining the flower's contour. Do not use the pointed stick in this case or you will destroy the sand mound before the flower is in place. Proceed with the covering process described earlier.

When preserving very small flowers, such as forget-me-nots, you may process as many as you can get in the container without crowding them. The procedure here would be to cut the stems short enough so that the flower heads are well covered when the box is full of sand. However, do not use an extremely shallow container, but select one that is deep enough to allow at least three inches of stem to remain on the flowers. After they are dried, they can be bunched together and taped around a longer stem or wire, before they are placed in the arrangement, which is the most effective way to display them. Other small flowers such as aubretia, sweet alyssum, violets, creeping buttercups, and so forth, can be preserved in the same way.

The grace and beauty of the mock orange is best preserved in spray form. This means that both flowers and foliage are preserved at one time. If the spray is not too long, it should be processed face up. But you will need a rather large and tall container so that you will have sufficient room to work with the covering and at the same time not crowd the spray. The preservation of a spray of multiple forms, such as this, requires a thorough working knowledge of the technique, along with a swift and deft touch; therefore, it should not be attempted until some experience has been acquired.

## Covering the Flower

### Face-Down Position

This method, though not used as often as the face-up technique, is practical for such flowers as the cosmos, clematis, certain varieties of the bluebell family where the open bells point downward, and others. I sometimes use it for small lateral sprays of delphinium and larkspur, because it saves time, sand and space.

The face-down position allows you to reduce the amount of sand in the bottom of the container, because there is no stem to be supported in the sand. But you do need a liberal sprinkling of sand at the bottom, about one-quarter inch, enough to keep the flower petals from touching the container. Hold the flower by its stem with the face of the bloom pointed downward and resting gently on this thin cushion. As with the face-up position, start with the inner edges of the container and work toward the flower. When the bloom becomes securely anchored, you may release the stem as you finish covering the flower. Apply the

For tall flower, add collar just before container is full. Continue adding sand until the flower is covered.

sand just as you would in the face-up method. Your pointed stick is necessary only to straighten a tangled petal here and there. The container should be tapped for air pockets, labeled and set away to dry. Small lateral sprays of delphinium may be covered in this manner provided you have a deep enough container. Two-quart milk cartons or tall juice cans will answer the purpose. When you use such a deep container, it becomes quite impossible for you to observe what you are doing, at least at the beginning of the procedure. I have developed a system which, if carefully followed, will insure good results whether you can see what you are doing or not. I call it the "Faith" method.

### The "Faith" Method

Hold the flower spike by the stem, with the hand near the last row of florets. Point the spray face down in the container, allowing the tip to rest gently on the sand cushion. Brace the little finger on the edge of the container while holding the stem with

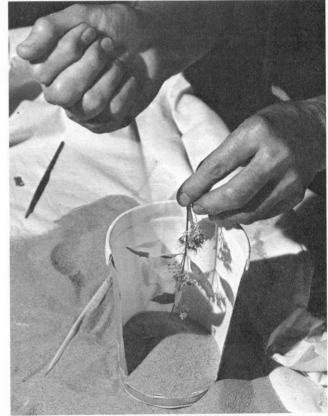

To preserve flower face down, hold it by the stem, with face of bloom resting on ¼-inch layer of sand.

the thumb and index finger. This supports and steadies the flower spike while it is being covered. Grasp a handful of sand with your free hand and let it flow evenly around the inside edge of the container. Then let another handful run down through the center of the flower spike as close to the central stem as possible. Keep repeating this procedure until the container is filled. Thus you will equalize the pressure on the inside and outside of each attached floret and get perfect results. If a portion of the flower still remains uncovered after the container is filled, tap all around for air pockets, then add a cardboard collar, and finish covering the flower. Label the container and set aside to dry. (See the work pictures illustrating this method; also Chapter Six, "Containers.")

The face-down method is valuable for such flowers as the cosmos and clematis, when you wish to preserve their graceful cup-like shape and also protect the bunched stamens in the centers. To do this, make a volcano-like mound, as was described in the face-up method. Then, with the tip of your little finger, make a depression in the top of the mound, deep enough to receive the stamen cluster without crushing them. You must use care in doing this to prevent the breaking down of the even outer line of the mound, because you are dependent on a uniform surface to preserve the contour of your flower. Place the stamens in the small depression that you have made, letting the petals fall over the sides of the mound. If the petals don't touch the sand, the mound is too pointed. Start over and make a larger mound, using more sand, until the petals rest naturally and closely to its sides.

The clematis is done in the same way except that there is usually a sudden flare of the lower tips of the petals downward. To preserve this graceful contour, place the stamens in the depression at the top of the cone, then gradually build up the sand under the tips of the petals both inside and out until they are well anchored. Then finish covering the flower.

### Horizontal Position

This position is best suited to long sprays, spikes and stalks. The spray is placed on its side in the container in about the same position that it would assume if you were to lay it down on a table. You will usually need a specially constructed box to fit the flower.

This method is the trickiest of all in that the flower being treated is usually made up of individual florets along a main stem. Or it consists of a maze of tiny blossoms, each of which must be covered individually while held in its natural position —and all must be done before the flower withers. This method is definitely not recommended for the beginner.

When the flower spray and container are ready, cover the bottom of the box with an inch of sand. Then cut three pieces of cardboard so that each is about three inches long and one-half inch wide. In one end of each tab, cut a V-shaped notch an inch deep. Place the tabs with the PRONGS UP in the sand, one in the middle, the other two at the ends and about three inches from the ends of the container. (You may have to build up more sand around each tab to support them properly.) Lay the stalk or spray of flowers in the box, making sure that the central stem rests in the notch of each tab. The cardboard supports will be sufficient to hold the spray in place while it is being covered, will prevent flattening of any side branches or florets, and will provide room to treat the flowers underneath without disturbing their natural position.

Starting from the far edge, let the sand flow from your hand and work toward the flowers, distributing it evenly in the middle and along the sides. Work on the lowest flowers first. Your pointed stick can be used to manipulate a stubborn flower to a slightly better position so that it can be covered more easily. As you cover each floret, alternate the stream of sand in front and back to prevent distortion. Keep your sandbed level as you proceed until the spray is covered and the box is full. Speed is necessary but do not sacrifice technique. When you have finished, label the box and set it aside to dry.

One special caution: Do not try to lift a large, full container. The weight may cause either your back or the box to collapse. If the box is extremely large, spread a bed sheet or plastic covering on the floor where you wish your spray to remain while it dries. You can do your covering with the container on the sheet,

Flower to be preserved in a horizontal position is supported by V-shaped tabs of cardboard in sand.

and a bucket of sand nearby. Later, when you uncover the flower, you can easily retrieve the sand that falls on the sheet and save wear and tear on muscle and bone.

The preservation of extremely tall stalks of delphinium is difficult, for it is not easy to find or even construct a container long enough to accommodate them. And there is always the chance that they will wither, no matter how rapidly you work, before you can finish covering them. The best procedure is to cut the entire stalk and place the stem in cold water. Then cut the top third and process it horizontally. When that is done, cut off the second third and proceed in the same way. The last third receives the same treatment.

The proper assembling, when the flower is done, presents no serious problem, since all delphinium stems are hollow. Take as many flat toothpicks as are necessary to fill the stem cavity without breaking it, and dip the ends of the toothpicks in acetate cement. Starting with the top third of the plant, push the picks into the stem, leaving the bottom half of the picks protruding. Now dip the free ends of the picks in cement and insert them into the top stem of the second section of the flower. Press the sections together until the ends of the flower stems meet. The joint will be invisible, even to you. Then, using the same procedure, join the third section to the rest of the plant. It is possible thus to preserve a specimen of spectacular size and height without sacrificing any of its pristine beauty. (See the work picture of the horizontal method.)

## Summary

Every flower that you will process will be done in one of these three basic positions. If you use sand, the drying time for most flowers will be two weeks. But they may be left in the sand indefinitely with no harmful results. The containers should be set in a warm dry place. An attic is ideal, but a clothes closet will do. In a dry climate the basement is adequate and probably will be the most convenient place in which to do all of your work. I dry, store and conduct classes in mine.

The hot summer is best for this work and the flowers don't mind if the temperature climbs above 100°. True, they dry sooner in very hot weather, but since you may leave them in the sand as long as you like, you need not rush to open them. In fact, I advise waiting the full two weeks.

During spring and fall and in damp weather, the drying takes a little longer, but you will never have to cover the containers. And the sand does not require "drying out" before reusing.

If desiccants other than sand are used, the timing will be different. Silica gel requires only one week for drying, and devotees of the cornmeal and borax method advocate different drying periods for different flowers. They do warn, however, that over-drying tends to burn and this may affect the colors of the flowers.

One final word of caution: In your unbounded enthusiasm (which I know you will develop), don't place so many containers around you that you find yourself hemmed in. How often have I done just that, expecting to move them later! Invariably the doorbell or telephone rings and I have been forced to make a jump for it to extricate myself, and usually with tragic results. Also leave a clear path somewhere on the basement floor so that the gas man can get through to read the meter. Every time a new man comes to read my gas meter, he turns very pale, peeks at me out of the corner of his eye and always manages to keep a sizeable distance from me at all times.

# CHAPTER X

# Uncovering and Cleaning the Flower

Any flower preserver's first experiment will be one of the longest two weeks ever spent—the two weeks the bloom is in the sand. The strongest warning that I can give is: control your curiosity! Only when the full allotted time has elapsed may a peek be taken at the buried flower.

And heed well this admonition and do as I say—not as I sometimes do, for I confess that impatience is one of my worst enemies. Very often when I am experimenting with a new flower, I keep trying to justify a tiny peek to see how it is really going to look. I keep telling myself that perhaps this one flower has a very small water content or perhaps the weather has been warm enough to speed up the drying. Too often I weaken and take a peek, and the sad and inevitable result is always the same. The flower flops. So I hope that I am right in assuming that your will power is greater than mine, and that you will wait until the full time for dehydration has elapsed before you start to uncover.

The moment of uncovering your first flower will be one of the thrilling moments in your life. After all, you are a flower lover or you wouldn't be doing this work in the first place. The excitement of being able to preserve a flower, figuratively speaking, forever, and seeing it emerge from the desiccant, always causes the pulse to beat a bit faster. I constantly hear little squeals of delight from my pupils as they uncover their first flower. One student looked up helplessly, but happily, and exclaimed, "I think I am going to have a heart attack!" So in order to enjoy this moment to its fullest, I repeat, let the flower dry the full time it needs—from one to four weeks. (See Chapter XVIII, "Encyclopedia of Flowers and Their Special Treatment.")

## *How to Uncover the Flower*

If you have used the face-up method, hold the container in the left hand and slowly tip it sideways, allowing the sand to fall into the mother box. Hold the other hand, fingers spread apart, over the box as the sand is poured. Do not stop pouring even though a petal may fall, because any sudden reverse motion of the sand could dislodge other petals, thus causing more damage. In the event this does happen, quickly transfer the container to another point over the mother box until you can pick up the petal before it becomes lost in the sand. The fallen petal, thus retrieved, can be put back on the flower later with a bit of glue. When the container is emptied, let the flower fall face forward, gently, into the palm of the right hand. Lay the empty container down and pick up the flower by its stem—never by its petals. It will be mottled with grains of sand which you can remove later. From here on and until a flower is in the final arrangement, it must never be laid on its side on the floor or on a table, but must be placed upright. Otherwise, it may be damaged.

Hold hand with fingers spread apart in front of container when uncovering flower in the face-up position.

For flower in face-down position, proceed as with face-up flower but grasp stem when it appears.

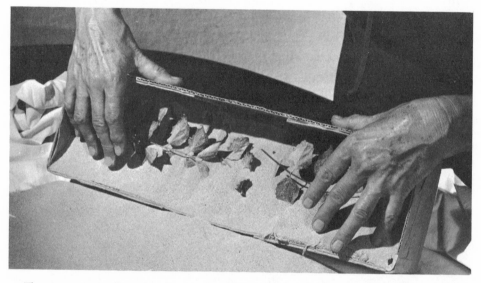

To uncover a plant in the horizontal position, tip sand onto cloth while protecting plant with hands.

### Storage of Preserved Blooms

I have discarded the old-fashioned way of storing dried specimens in boxes, shelves and racks for a more convenient and space-saving method. As you progress in the art of preserving flowers, you will be carried away by your enthusiasm; you will want to dry every new flower that you see. But where to put them becomes an ever perplexing question. This happened to me. I tried placing flowers on specially constructed racks, shelves and in boxes, but found that I could accommodate more than ten times as many flowers when I placed them in temporary stems and inserted the stems in a container of sand than I could when they were spread out, individually, over a given area, and with better protection to the flowers. Another drawback was that the racks had to be made of a coarsely meshed material, or holes had to be punched through a solid surface in order to accommodate the stems. Even so, it is wise to curb your enthusiasm somewhat or you may find yourself literally stemmed in.

I now slip the flower stems temporarily into dried stems and stand them upright in a container of unwashed sand. (Don't use your washed sand for this; the unwashed will do just as well.) Thus, by using a variety of stem lengths I can put as many in as the container will hold, provided they are not crowded and that they do not touch one another. In addition, when I am making an arrangement I can see all the colors and forms that I have on hand to choose from.

You should accumulate a good supply of stems of varying lengths and thicknesses. Daisy stems are excellent because they are hollow. But any stem will do as long as it has a soft center which can be made hollow by piercing it with the small end of a toothpick. Always be on the lookout for good stems. The average countryside is a gold mine and your garden will give you more than you may suspect.

Preparing them is simple. Just shear off the leaves and let the stems dry. It is a good idea to provide a special long box for stems. Keep the box constantly replenished. When you cut, buy, or are given flowers, you can save the unused portions of stems for your collection. Don't neglect the tiny ones; you will need many.

Flowers covered face down are uncovered in the same way as those buried face up, except that the process is a little easier. You will expose the stem first and you can hold that until you are finished.

With flowers buried horizontally, place the container length-wise in the mother box, tip it sideways and allow the sand to flow out gently. Before the flower has been stored after covering, it is well to mark which end of the container holds the cut end of the stem. Thus you can be ready to grasp the cut end as it emerges. Get a good grip on it, because the larger the box the greater the pressure behind the flower coming out.

Of course, the very long container holding the horizontal flower cannot be moved; it must be emptied on the sheet or plastic upon which it is resting. See that there is a sufficient amount of cloth beyond the container to catch and hold the sand when the box is emptied. Tip the box sideways, letting the sand fall slowly onto the cloth. As the stem emerges, grasp it at the end and continue holding on to it until the entire flower is uncovered. The sand can be retrieved later and added to your sand supply.

### Cleaning the Flower

Your cleaning materials will include several camel's hair brushes of different sizes. They can usually be bought at any dime store or at an art supply center, but they must be soft and fine-textured. Also included should be a package of flat toothpicks, scissors, a tube of clear acetate cement, a bottle of fingernail polish remover or acetone, and an empty nail polish bottle with a cap and brush attached and an eye dropper.

First prepare the glue. The petals of many flowers will shatter unless they are reinforced with cement and allowed to dry before they are cleaned.

### Preparing the Glue

To prepare the glue, squeeze acetate cement into a small, empty fingernail polish bottle until it is almost half full. Now pour in clear nail polish remover or acetone until the bottle is just a little less than full. Then screw on the cap with the small brush attached and shake the bottle until the ingredients are thoroughly mixed. The polish remover will dilute the cement, thus allowing the solution to seep quickly down to the base of the petals. It also prevents the shine that undiluted glue leaves. The solution dries in about five minutes.

## Uncovering and Cleaning the Flower

I have often been asked why I do not use a water-based glue or mucilage. I have found that these cements tend to "bead" on the petals and do not penetrate to the base of the flower as the diluted acetate glue does. Furthermore, they take longer to dry than the other one does.

It is possible that you may not be able to obtain the small bottle of fingernail polish with the brush attached, or you might find it more convenient to use an ordinary bottle because it will hold more. The results will be the same, and instead of using the small brush, you may use the medicine dropper to drip your glue.

Several months ago I found a new type of glue in a hobby shop that I prefer to the kind described above for the following reasons: It is ready mixed and of the right consistency, does not leave a white stain on the flower (the acetate solution sometimes stains a dark petal surface), dries quickly and comes in a plastic bottle with its own pouring spout attached. I suspect that it is a plastic product and therefore might even be used on fresh flowers, although I have not tested it out in this capacity as yet. It is called Clear Glue and is manufactured by Snow Foam Products, Inc., El Monte, California. It costs 89 cents for a four ounce bottle. I suggest that you try it.

In case you are unable to obtain this product, you can still mix your own and, if mixed with care, it will give you good results. I have used it during all of my years of flower drying. Hereafter, throughout the book, the reference to diluted glue can mean either kind.

WARNING: *Diluted glue is for reinforcing only. Use glue · straight from the tube when gluing fallen petals back on.*


### Cleaning Technique

There is an advantage in cleaning the flower as soon as it is taken out of the sand. The petals are more flexible at this time than they will be later on and there is always an immediate pleasure in seeing the finished product, clean and free from adhering particles of the desiccant. But if you do not have the time to do it, you can store them away and wait for another day.

Pick up the flower by the stem with the flower head pointing downward. Gently tap the stem with a pencil or your pointed stick. This frees the flower of the loose grains of sand that are lodged in the center and through the petals. You will be amazed at the amount of sand that falls. You must do this gently and carefully, especially if the flower has many petals, or you will dislodge them. An even greater danger could be to the centers, so use the utmost care in performing this operation.

## Reinforcing with Glue

If a flower needs reinforcing, do the following before you clean it. Hold the flower face up in one hand. With the nail polish brush, transfer the diluted glue quickly to its center. If you prefer, you may use the medicine dropper to do this. Hold the brush directly over the stamens and let the glue drip as it will. Repeat the application several times. The flower may be tipped slightly, first in one direction, then in another, to make sure that the glue reaches its heart. Then place the flower upright in a can of sand until it dries, about five minutes.

To glue flower from top, hold it face up and drip diluted glue into it from brush.

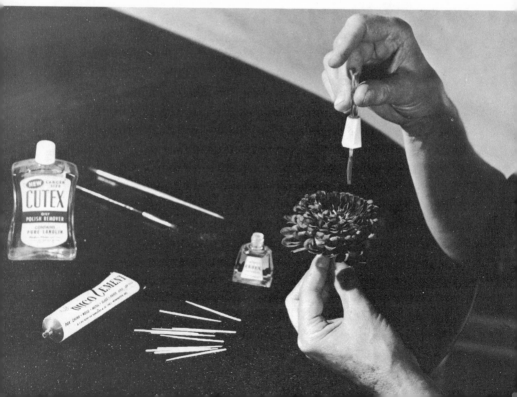

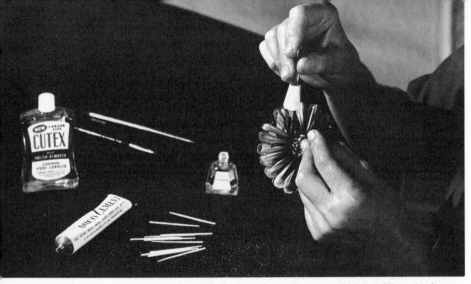

To glue flower from bottom, hold flower face down and drip diluted glue into it from brush as shown.

Sand is removed from uncovered flower with camel's hair paintbrush. Toothpicks are for stubborn grains.

Again pick the flower up by its stem. Then using the large end of a flat toothpick (round ones won't do), scrape off all the grains of sand. Begin with the calyx, sepals and underpetals. A very light touch usually does the trick; you must learn to use a feather-light touch in all handling of flowers. Next, give the sand-free surfaces a light brushing with one of the camel's hair brushes.

‡‡ 83 ‡‡

The next step is to turn the flower face up so that the inside can be cleaned in the same way. Do not forget to dislodge any grains of sand that may be clinging to the stamens. When the flower is clean and smooth, give it a light spraying with the moisture-proofing spray. The complete directions for spraying will be found on the spray can. Follow them carefully. After the final spray is applied, you may insert your flower in the sand container and forget about it until you are ready to apply its permanent stem and use it in an arrangement. This new spray is the best one that I have ever used. It is called "Moistureproofing Spray." It comes in a 13-ounce spray can and costs $2.50. It can be purchased from Flowers and Crafts, Heritage Square, Golden, Colorado 80401. It will be referred to many times throughout the book, for various purposes.

After your flower is cleaned, and if it was dyed before you buried it in the desiccant, go over the petals with a light brushing to make sure the chalk is all removed. Then give it a light spraying with the moisture-proofing spray. This will appear to alter the color somewhat while it is still damp. You must wait until the spray is completely dry before you decide whether it needs another application of color or not. If it does, apply the powdered chalk with a brush, on each petal, being sure to remove the excess before giving it the second coat of spray. If the flower type is such that brushing is impracticable or impossible, the chalk may be sifted over the flower while it is being rotated. A gentle tapping or light sandblasting will remove the excess chalk in this case.

The composite (a flower head composed of many small petals or flowers) family of flowers requires special treatment when uncovering and cleaning. The aster is an example. Uncover the flower very slowly and carefully or it will shatter. The impossibility of ever gluing this multitude of petals back on the flower is evident. But if you can remove it from the sand without breaking it, it is advisable to reinforce the petals from underneath, where the lower row of petals is joined to the center. Do this by gently lifting the lower row upwards, a few at a time, and letting the diluted glue drip into the base of the flower. Hold in this position for a few minutes in order to let the glue seep through the center of the cone, and set. Do this all the way around the flower. Then turn it face up and add a few drops of glue at the base of the top petals. Set it upright to dry. Then you may proceed with the cleaning. The same procedure can be followed with the dahlia, African marigold, chrysanthemum, and others of this double variety.

The carnation needs special care also, but of a slightly different kind. You will notice that the petals rattle around in the dried flower. This is because of the shrinkage in the petal fibers which run down through the elongated calyx. To correct this, separate the petals slightly and hold them apart at the top while you let a generous amount of the diluted glue drip down through them to the calyx.

Tip the flower in every direction in order to make sure the glue is evenly distributed inside of the calyx. Then gently force the petals together by closing your fingers around the calyx. Hold in this position a few minutes until dry. Or you may wrap the calyx, firmly, with several strands of thread which can be removed when the glue has dried.

The single daisy has its own problems. I have often said, "Show me a person who can dry a daisy perfectly and I will show you a good flower preserver." The chief problem here seems to be with the yellow centers. They often separate when taken from the sand. The first time I dried them, upon observing this, I concluded that tiny insects, hiding in the centers, had eaten them. This is not an impossible supposition. So before you put them in the sand, be sure to give the stems a severe tapping to remove these minute creatures that are usually found in the hearts of fresh daisies.

The separation of the center segments, however, is another matter, not because of insects, but because of the shrinkage of the green sepals on the back of the flower. You will notice that the yellow centers are still soft and pliable, to a degree, if you have not left them too long in the sand. At this stage, they can be re-formed into their original solid mass with a sharp pointed stick or with a toothpick. It is best to start from their outer edge and gently push them together toward the center. This will restore them to their original position and they will remain so until they are solid. A light dabbing with yellow powdered chalk will restore and keep their fresh yellow color.

The zinnia has the reputation of being a coarse-textured flower. Whether or not you choose to dye it before processing, you will find that an additional brushing with colored chalk of the same color as the flower will restore the velvety texture of the petals.

The rose is a complete saga in itself and will be dealt with in all of its stages of bloom in Chapter XVIII, "Encyclopedia of Flowers and Their Special Treatment."

## Protection of Preserved Material

In a dry climate, dried flowers need no protection except during prolonged damp weather when the house is not being heated. During rainy spells, I put various receptacles, each holding a handful or two of silica gel, around the basement. This chemical quickly absorbs the moisture in the atmosphere. When it is saturated, it turns pink. It must then be dried out in the oven until its original blue color is restored and it can be reused indefinitely. You can purchase silica gel at any chemical store. However, if you cannot obtain this material, an electric heater turned on for a few hours daily will do the job.

Spring, fall and winter present no particular problems in most localities because whenever the furnace is on, it dries out the air and your flowers are safe. But protecting your flowers is not so simple in humid areas. Day to day protection will not do. As of this writing, the best way to protect flowers permanently is by means of a chemical spray, already referred to in this chapter.

## How to Keep Them Clean

There are three ways to keep preserved flowers clean. The only treatment necessary for those with large petal surfaces is a light brushing with a camel's hair brush. Others can have their freshness restored by a light sandblasting. To do this, sift clean sand over them as you rotate their stems. Reach all surfaces. The sand will bounce off carrying the accumulated dust with it. Or you may dip them, one at a time, in any good dry-cleaning fluid. Of course, this method does not apply to dyed flowers nor to flowers already made up in an arrangement. It applies only to the stock on hand that you may wish to freshen up a bit before making the arrangement.

There are a few general rules that can be observed by anyone, whether she is the originator or the purchaser: Delicate fine sprays or flowers rarely ever attract or show the dust and it is a good thing that they don't, because they would not tolerate brushing; the only way they could be cleaned would be to remove them from the arrangement and give them a light sandblasting and this is unthinkable. As I said before, however, any dust that might be there is invisible, so leave them alone. Even medium-sized or large flowers seldom show a film if they are light in color. It is the large dark flowers that cause concern. Here, even a slight coating is noticeable. The only safe and practical way to clean them is with a soft camel's hair brush. Gently brush them, one petal at a time. Support the petal from the underside with your finger or with a thin strip of cardboard as you brush so that the pressure will not dislodge the petal being cleaned. Make sure the dust is removed from the brush from time to time as it accumulates. I usually dip my brush in cooking oil, wipe it dry, and then proceed with the brushing. The dust seems to cling to a slightly oiled brush more than to a dry one, which is precisely what I want. But it is necessary to clean the brush more often.

Foliage, unless it is of the fern variety, can be cleaned in the same way.

Do not experiment with the vacuum cleaner as so many people eagerly suggest. You will have no flowers left if you do. Wind, in any form, is their enemy.

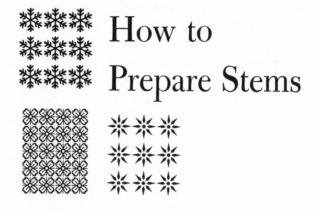

# CHAPTER XI

# How to Prepare Stems

As we have seen most flowers are removed from their original stalks before being preserved. It is now time to consider the subject of stems for the finished flower—the various kinds, where to collect them, their treatment, the permanent assembly of stem and flower, along with the accompanying necessary grooming and good tailoring.

Among the first things to do when you begin preserving flowers is to start a collection of stems. You will need all kinds, lengths, and thicknesses. Any place in the countryside is abundant with weeds; in many cases, these provide the best stems of all. But you will be amazed at the number and varieties that your own garden will provide.

Stems should be chosen with the following characteristics in mind: They must have hollow centers; if not hollow, at least soft enough so they can be made to receive a wire or flower stem, by piercing the cut end with a toothpick. They should be chosen for their sturdiness and strength. Nothing is more disconcerting than to prepare a stem for a flower and then suddenly have it collapse between your fingers. They should also be of varying sizes, from the very thickest to the very thinnest. These tiny ones are usually found on plants as smaller branches or laterals and should never be discarded or ignored. They will prove to be the most valuable of all because a large majority of flowers have small, delicate stems and stems that are added to these flowers should match them in size as nearly as possible. So collect all sizes and kinds and never again throw one away without first examining it with an eye to its use in your flower work.

I like daisy stems best of all, and I use and reuse them constantly. They have all of the necessary requirements for stem extensions of every method. Every conscientious gardener cuts down his daisies after each blooming period is over. If these are saved, your worries should be over. If you don't raise them in your own garden, ask your neighbor who does to save them for you. Larkspur and feverfew are also valuable, especially the small laterals, which provide a multitude of smaller stems.

Their preparation is simple. Just shear or pull off the leaves and stack the stems in a warm place to dry. They require no further treatment. But I suggest that you provide a long, deep box to keep them in. Thus, they are always ready and can be added to from time to time.

There will be times, however, when a straight long stem will not answer your purpose, either to use alone, such as a line in your arrangement, or as a base upon which to attach flowers. In such cases, it would be preferable to select a portion of a branch from a shrub or a tree, rather than a flower stem. After you have cut it and while it is still fresh and flexible, determine the curve that you wish it to assume and wrap strings or threads around it to hold it in place until it dries. Unless it has accompanying foliage, it does not need the sand treatment.

There is a definite trend today in contemporary flower arranging toward the use of such manipulated material and the outlines are often bold and imposing. Indeed, some nurseries offer shrubs that are grown for just such use. Harry Lauder's Walking Stick is a shrub whose branches are twisted and turned, almost like a walking stick, and which grows six to eight feet tall. Another is the Fan-Tail Willow. It is described as the decorator's and arranger's delight. The reason is that the shrub cannot decide which way to grow, so twists and curls in all directions.

It is not always possible to foresee your future needs and demands during the growing season and you may find that you have a specific need for a curved branch or stem that you failed to prepare in advance, while the material was fresh and flexible. The situation is not hopeless even though your material is dry and stiff; it can still be curved and altered to suit your demands.

This is done by holding the stem over a pan of boiling water, subjecting it to a steam bath for about five or ten minutes. It will soften to the extent that it can be bent in a curve. But the stem must be fastened securely with a string until it is dry, or it will flop back to its original straight line.

Then there are the standards or simulated trunks of the foliage and flower trees. I purchase manzanita branches for the latter. Manzanita is preferable to ordinary dried branches because these may contain termites and manzanita is never infected by such creatures. The standards for miniature, eye level, and foliage trees can be made from a rose cane or other stem of substantial proportions. Choose a thick stem that is long and straight.

Carnation stems are unique, having markings and a color all their own. The finished flower always looks better when the real stems are applied to them rather than wires or other stems. So conserve the stems of carnations and pinks if you plan to dry the flowers.

The extensions of stems for very small flowers, such as the violet, forget-me-not, buttercup, and so forth, should be of very fine wire. They are more effective in an arrangement if they are bunched together. This requires a flexibility that dried stems do not possess. The method of applying such stems will be discussed later on in this chapter.

## Materials Needed for Stems

Besides a good collection of real stems, you will require some wire. I prefer the kind that is wrapped with green thread; it is easier to work with. I suggest that you buy one pound of 18-gauge for large flowers, a pound of 20-gauge for smaller ones and a bunch or two of very fine wire for small flowers. You must have a spool of green floral tape, toothpicks, a wire cutter, pins, a tube of acetate cement, paint for the stems, and a series of camel's hair brushes of varying sizes.

All of these materials can be purchased at a good hobby shop or paint store with the exception of the toothpicks and wire cutter. You probably have these items around the house; if not, get them at a hardware store. I buy two kinds of paint: an artist's oil paint and also the new acrylic variety. If you follow my example you will purchase four tubes of each because sometimes you will prefer the oil base; at other times, the acrylic, which is mixed with water. The colors should consist of dark green, yellow, white and burnt sienna. All these colors are available in both kinds of paint. Have on hand a bottle of turpentine, two empty bottles with screw tops and some water.

## Mixing the Paint

The oil paint is mixed in the following way: squeeze about two inches of green into a medium-sized glass bottle (not plastic). Add a pea-sized amount of yellow, half this amount of white, and a speck of burnt sienna. Pour in approximately three tablespoons of turpentine. Screw on the lid and shake the bottle until the colors are thoroughly mixed.

It must be understood that this is not the ultimate formula for all greens, stems or foliage. It is meant to be simply a base from which to begin. Be critical. Study the green carefully and make your paint correspond to it. If your stem or leaf is of a pale spring green, use more yellow and white. If it is of a dark evergreen shade, use very little of these two colors but use more dark green and a bit more burnt sienna or umber. Even the consistency may not be suitable for the material at hand. For general painting of stems and leaves, it should be of the consistency of a thin cream soup and, of course, every time you add more paint you must also thin with more turpentine. Then there are times when nothing but a very thin wash is desired, such as when painting the calyx of a hollyhock or the foliage of a moss rose. A little experience and a critical eye will soon teach you how to match your paints with the materials at hand.

The amounts of acrylic paint are the same except that you omit the turpentine. Use nothing except plain water to thin them. The amount of water will depend on how thick you want the paint. The best plan is to start out with a little and add more as you need it. In this case, the consistency should be about the same as a syrup. There is an acrylic polymer emulsion, named Polymer Medium, which can be added to your acrylic paint;

it produces a shine, and the degree of the shine is controlled by the amount of the emulsion that is added.

Never dip the brush into the bottle but, rather, pour a small amount of paint into a metal bottle cap and work from this. All stems of single flowers whether real or wrapped with tape should be painted. Sprays are different. They may or may not be painted, depending on the stem and your own choice. When painting, don't neglect the calyx and sepals, both of which will benefit from a light brushing with paint. Return the unused paint to the bottle. If you cap the bottle tightly, the paint will keep indefinitely.

## Ways to Join Stems and Flowers

There are four different ways to attach stems to flowers: with (1) natural stems, (2) wire, (3) pins, or (4) a combination of both wire and stem.

1. Select a dried stem of any length but slightly larger in circumference than the stem of the flower. If the stem you select is not hollow, use the small end of a flat toothpick to make a hole in its top center. With a toothpick, put a dab of undiluted glue on the end of the flower stem and slip it into the hole. If the hole is the right size, the stem will go in easily, yet fit tightly. Next, paint the entire stem. This is the simplest method and is best for flowers which will be placed upright in an arrangement.

2. If the flower has an unusually large hollow stem, as does the zinnia or African marigold, do not use the first method which would require a base stem so thick that the resulting combination would be ungainly. Rather, select a stem slightly smaller than the one on the flower. Apply glue to the base stem and slip it into the flower stem. Instead of a natural base stem, you may use a wire. But should the wire be too narrow for the opening of the flower stem, wrap the end of the wire with a small length of floral tape, apply glue, and insert it into the flower stem. Wrap the joint with floral tape to cover up any unevenness. Be sure to wrap the entire wire stem and paint it.

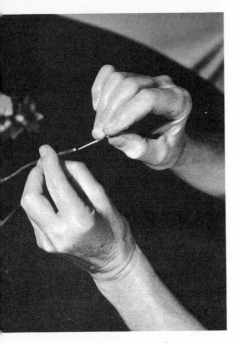

To add base stem to the stem on preserved flower, make hole in base stem with wire, toothpick, or pin.

Flower and base stem of equal size are joined with a toothpick. Holes are made before preserving.

Flower stem is fitted into hole of base stem. Drop of acetate cement will make the joint more solid.

If flower has unusually large hollow stem, insert base stem into flower and reinforce with glue.

WARNING: *Never wrap a real stem with floral tape, but always wrap a wire stem.* It makes no difference whether the wire is already enclosed in green thread or is bare; it must still be taped. There are two reasons for this: first, the tape helps cover up any obvious joints and gives a greater appearance of reality; second, the flower will not stay put in the arrangement unless it is wrapped.

Wrapping a real stem would be like gilding the lily, but both real and wire stems should be painted. The abrupt change of color where the stems meet shows up in the joint. So paint the entire stem one color from calyx to bottom.

A little practice is necessary before you can do an effective job of wrapping wire stems. It is largely a matter of concentrating on what each hand is doing at the same time. This is a time when the right hand must know what the left hand doeth.

Each flower arranger develops his own special technique. Here is mine.

Start with the end of the tape in one hand. Hold it in front of and against the stem, a little above the point where the stem and wire meet. Pressing with the thumb and forefinger, roll it around the stem. The movement of the thumb is always forward toward the tip of the third finger. As you proceed, use your free hand to stretch the tape downward and slightly to one side of the wire. Continue until the wire has been covered to the very end. Pinch off the excess tape. Now run the thumb and index finger along the entire stem to smooth out any wrinkles. If your wrapping is still loose, you failed to apply enough pressure while you were twirling the tape around the flower.

3. If you wish to join the flower to its original stem, as with roses or carnations, you can do so quickly and easily. Before preserving the flower, insert a pin in the piece of stem still attached to it. Cut off the pin leaving about one-half inch embedded in the flower stem (see Chapter IX, "Covering the Flower"). Also remember that any stem with foliage remaining on it must be preserved in a drying medium (see Chapter XII, "Ways to Preserve Foliage"). At the time you cut the flower

head from the main stem and insert the pin, a similar pin shold be slipped into the cut end of the original stem before it is dried. When the flower and original stem are ready to be assembled, pull the pin out of the long stem with pliers. A hole will be left to receive the pin already anchored in the flower section. Apply cement to this pin and insert it into the hole. The result is a strong indiscernible joint. Thus it is possible to) preserve roses and other flowers with foliage and long stems intact. (For detailed instructions on drying and assembling flower clusters, see chapter on "Covering the Flower.")

4. The last method of applying stems is the most complicated. It is my favorite method, however, because it meets the needs of more types of flowers and it also conserves my stockpile of stems. I would rather invest in more wire than deplete my stem supply. Then, too, most flowers have stems too small and brittle to permit inserting a wire. They can, however, be given a real stem of appropriate size according to the simple method described above. But, again, in this case the stem would remain upright and stiff.

You may require a curved line, so this method won't do. Alter it as follows: Proceed by selecting a natural stem whose circumference is slightly greater than the stem of the flower. Press it between the fingers; if it yields to the pressure discard it and select a stronger one. Sturdiness is required for this operation. Insert the flower stem (with glue) as directed. Next cut the main stem, leaving about an inch of it attached to the flower stem. Select a wire of desired length and unwind the thread for about a half inch. Cut off the unwound thread close to the wire. Dip the exposed wire in glue and insert it in the stem end. Push it up toward the flower. Wrap the wire stem as indicated and finish by painting it green.

Both wire and natural stems can be shortened with a wire cutter. They can be lengthened by inserting them in natural stems of greater circumference. Make sure the added stem is sturdy enough to withstand the weight.

# CHAPTER XII

# Ways to Preserve Foliage

Mother Nature must have loved the green things of this world —she made so many of them. The need for a varied and abundant supply of foliage is as important to the flower preserver as flowers are. Foliage in a bouquet is what a frame is to a picture. As a matter of fact, many types of foliage should be preserved for their own sakes because they can be striking and decorative even without a color accent. And they are certainly a necessary adjunct to any flower arrangement, be it dried or fresh.

The beginner tends to forget that all the foliage is usually stripped from the flower before it is preserved and therefore has to be replaced. It always takes more than you think it will to take to cover up the bare stems and to fill in those void spots. So be prepared to do as many varieties as you can collect because aside from fulfilling your needs, you never know just when you will see the need for one certain type of leaf or vine to make your arrangement outstanding.

Those people who live in tropical or semi-tropical areas are very fortunate indeed, because they have so many choices of year-round foliage that the temperate climates do not offer. Still, if we in the colder regions really take the trouble to search for beautiful foliage, we can always find more than enough to fill our needs.

There are perhaps seven ways to preserve foliage that are in practice today. These are (1) pressing under heavy weights, (2) causing the stems to absorb a glycerin and water solution, (3) immersing in a solution of the latter, (4) pressing with a warm iron, (5) air drying, (6) skeletonizing, and (7) burying in a dry desiccant. All have their particular merits at certain times, but except for these special cases that arise, I have found that the dry desiccant and the glycerin and water bath solution are most successful. It would be well to examine the merits and limitations of each method in turn.

The practice of pressing foliage between sheets of protective coverings and under heavy weights has long been the accepted procedure of most flower dryers. But foliage prepared in this way has never had any more appeal to me than a pressed flower has. It is flat, uninteresting and lacking in the natural grace and curves with which nature endowed it. And there is just as much need for the preservation of these characteristics in foliage as there is in flowers. One improperly done can ruin the looks of the other. So I ruled out this method from the very beginning.

Nor have I been satisfied with the results I obtained from attempting to preserve foliage by the stem absorption method. The accepted procedure is to cut the branch or stem, slit or hammer the end, and then submerge the stem in a warm solution of one-third glycerin and two-thirds water. A comparatively narrow container, such as a jar or glass bottle, will hold enough to accomplish the job. Little more than the cut or mashed portion of the stem need be submerged. The theory is that the solution will travel up the stem and penetrate in turn each leaf and cluster and eventually reach the top tip of the branch. Thus it is preserved.

My criticism of this method is that the tip and top portions of the branch wither before the solution ever reaches them, and as the top is the most conspicuous segment of the specimen, it shows up as just a plain wilted failure. There are those who even advocate spraying each leaf once a day with the glycerin solution to lessen the danger of this happening. My experience has been that even this is of little avail if the branch is much over a foot long. In any event, it is too much work and too uncertain to ensure the desired results. But you most assuredly will want to try this out and judge for yourself.

The immersion of the foliage in the glycerin and water solution is more certain and a great deal less work. It entails more initial expense but it can be used indefinitely from year to year. It will not preserve every type of foliage but those that are successful have certain qualities—notably long-lasting flexibility—that no other preserved foliage possesses.

The method that I use is to prepare a mixture of one-half water and one-half glycerin and mix it well in a large container, such as a plastic dishpan, crock, or other container of appropriate material. It should be large enough and full enough of the solution to accommodate the foliage without crowding. It is well to have on hand two or three large empty cans that can be set on top of the foliage after it is put in the solution to keep it from floating on top.

Each type of foliage requires a different length of time to reach the desired absorption stage. No foliage should be attempted until it has reached its full maturity, which would mean mid-summer and early fall. Heavy, coarse-textured material responds best to this treatment. Never attempt a delicate fern-like specimen; it will curl up and have to be discarded.

When the leaves are about two-thirds clear and translucent and darker than the green one-third of the leaf, the correct absorption stage has been reached. It is then advisable to remove all the foliage that is "done." If you discover some pieces that are still all green and opaque looking, replace them in the solution until such time as the absorption stage has been reached. In other words, a two-thirds absorption means that two-thirds of the leaf surface has turned dark and clear.

Lay the treated foliage that you have removed from the solution on several thicknesses of newspaper in a pile (not spread out) and allow them to remain there for several days. This is what I call a ripening time. They are drained of the excess solution, but an equalization of the absorbed juices takes place. The remaining green portion of the leaf is softened to the extent that the flexibility of the entire leaf is made permanent and will endure. If the foliage were kept longer in the solution, complete absorption would take place, of course, but the leaves would not possess enough rigidity to maintain their contour. They would flop.

After several days of this curing process have elapsed, wash the foliage in warm soapsuds and rinse in clear water. They may be placed in empty cans or bottles or hung up on a clothesline to dry. You will notice a marked change in color, ranging from a dark brownish green through tan to a dark brown, depending upon the type of foliage processed. You may use them as they are or spray them with green before using them in the arrangement. I prefer spraying all foliage after processing because I find that it is the only way to keep the natural green color indefinitely.

The two green sprays that I use and can recommend are (1) Fiddleleaf Green No. 720, Design Master, manufactured by Colorado Dye and Chemical Company, Inc., Boulder, Colorado. It is a dark green, suitable for many types of foliage such as peony leaves, boxwood, conifer family, holly and others. (2) Moss Green No. P-5, Aleene's Spray Paint, manufactured by Aleene, Temple City, California. It is a lighter green, suitable for ferns, rose foliage, fruit leaves, and so forth. Both sprays can be used on either glycerinized or sand-dried foliage. Both are available in most hobby shops.

Pressing flowers with a warm iron is useful in certain circumstances. It is probably the best way to preserve autumn leaves because it does preserve the flexibility and the color. They may not last as long as they would if preserved in a dry desiccant, but they do have more of that fresh look, and I have known people to keep them looking this way for at least two years.

The procedure is to put a piece of wax paper underneath and another on top of the leaf and run over the whole with a medium hot iron. The result is that a fine coating of wax encases the leaf and thus forms a protective coating on both sides of it. This must be done leaf by leaf with a new set of wax papers each time. Obviously this entails a great deal of time and labor, but if your appetite is strong enough for autumn leaves, the reward will be worth the labor.

## Ways to Preserve Foliage

A mildly warm iron is sometimes used on glycerinized leaves when they have become distorted in the solution by overcrowding and are a bit wrinkled. In every case, use a paper covering before pressing. In this way, many an error can be rectified and the branch can be restored to its pristine smoothness.

Air drying is simply hanging the material upside down on a clothesline to dry, or you may stand it upright in a container until it is conditioned. This process is used on ornamental grasses and certain types of woolly leaves such as lamb's ears, dusty miller, and so forth.

Skeletonizing is accomplished by softening and scraping away the soft tissues, thus reducing the leaf to its basic framework. It is a long and tedious process. I hesitate to recommend it because the danger of breaking the fibers is very great. Also, if you must have skeletonized leaves, they can be purchased in some Oriental stores, hobby shops and from some florists.

However, for those who would like to try their hand at it, here is the way to do it: Add about one tablespoon of lye to a quart of water and bring it to a boil. Simmer your leaves in it for about an hour (and they should be substantial in size and body). Rinse thoroughly and spread them out on a blotter or piece of paper toweling. Now the trick is to scrape off all of the softened tissue, using a dull blade of a knife, until only the skeleton or veins of the leaf are left. Some people advocate boiling them again in water containing bleach to whiten them. Others suggest dipping them in liquid dye for a desired color effect. You may take your choice. In either event, it is well to press them between a hard surface and heavy object until they are thoroughly dry and set in structure.

## Sand Drying Foliage

This is the method that you can depend upon to preserve foliage when every other method fails. Offhand, I know of no foliage that cannot be dried by this method. Furthermore, it is perhaps the only way by which every curve and original line of a piece of greenery can be preserved in its original form, be it a cluster or a single leaf.

Like every other method, however, it does have its short-comings. After emerging from the desiccant, the foliage is very brittle and unless it is of substantial body, great care must be used in placing it in the arrangement so that it doesn't break. There are some exceptions to this rule that will be mentioned later in this chapter when we consider individual specimens and kinds.

Covering the foliage with sand is comparatively easy and offers an exception to the rule of only one specimen to a container. You may put as many in a container as it will hold, provided there is a thin layer of sand between each piece and that pieces do not come into direct contact with one another or with the sides or bottom of the container. If many pieces are to be done, start with a moderately large container. Sprinkle about one-quarter inch of sand on the bottom. Now look over your collection and plan the space as economically as you can, but at the same time exercise great care in maintaining the natural position and curve of each piece. Flat leaves require a mere covering, but if the leaf is cupped, the hollow center must be supported and protected. Place the leaf over a small mound of sand. If a leaf is curved inward all along the central stem, as is the spirea, build up a long ridge and fit the curved leaf over it.

When you have used up all the space on the bottom layer, cover the leaves with sufficient sand to ensure a smooth, level bed upon which to start a second layer of foliage.

If a spray such as the Rosa hugonis is to be covered, let it rest naturally on the sand in a horizontal position. First cover the stems and leaves that are resting on the sand and then proceed to the next level. Build up the sand underneath each group of foliage in turn, then cover and proceed to groups higher up until you have covered the entire spray. Without disturbing or distorting the position of a single leaf or stem, cover each layer and start another until the box is filled. Tap the box for air pockets, label it, and set it away to dry. Allow two weeks if you use sand; one week if you use other media.

Uncover as for the face-up method, but be careful to remove each piece individually as it is uncovered. Add stems to sprays as you would add them to flowers. For instructions on the assembling of flowers on original stems and sprays, see Chapter XI, "How to Prepare Stems."

In my estimation, the maidenhair fern is the loveliest of all greenery. What a pity it will not last when cut; it is for this reason that florists do not stock it, at least in my area. It has largely been replaced by the leather fern in florists' work because the latter is longer lasting. However, your florist will order maidenhair fern for you. It is not overly expensive but you must consult with him as to the probable day and time of delivery and be prepared to take care of it as soon as it is delivered or you pick it up.

Have a box ready that will be large enough to accommodate a complete spray without crowding. It should measure twelve inches by twenty-four inches at a minimum and should be not more than six inches deep for easy handling. Maidenhair fern comes in bunches, but you will not be able to put it all in one box, so additional boxes should be ready and within reach.

When it arrives, take out about six sprays and put the remainder in the hydrator compartment of your refrigerator where you ordinarily keep salad greens. Put the stems of the sprays you have kept out in water and proceed with the covering.

Put a thin layer of sand on the bottom of the box, then lay a spray of the fern on it. Cover with sand and as you do so make sure that each tiny leaf is straight and flat so that there will be no distortions in the final product. One spray may be put on top of another provided there is a thin layer of sand between each. The reddish brown stems are flexible and can be bent in any direction you wish, as you proceed with the covering. When you have covered these first few, take a few more out of the refrigerator and process them in the same way, then a few more until they are all taken care of. The reason for this is that if you were to put them all in the water at one time, the last few would be curled and withered before you could attend to them. Do not put too many in one box because it would be too heavy to lift. Two weeks should be allowed for sand drying; one week if another desiccant is used.

Maidenhair fern will not tolerate the glycerin treatment. It will last for about six months without any additional care, but after that it does fade and turn white. I prefer to use mine in its natural coloring and then after the change in color has taken place, I remove it from the arrangement and spray it a moss green color. The stems and leaves are so lightweight and airy that I seldom insert them in the anchoring material, but simply slip them in between the flowers. Thus it is a small matter to remove them when they need this extra treatment.

The leaves of feverfew and thalictrum are similar to the maidenhair and have the same propensity to wither rapidly. In these cases it is also advisable to cut only a few leaves at a time and process them before cutting more. Again, like the maidenhair fern, they both resent the glycerin treatment. On the other hand, the leather fern almost demands the glycerin method. The dry desiccant leaves the spray dull and stiff, but it emerges from the wet solution glossy and flexible. True, the color is somewhat darker but not unlovely with certain combinations. However, it can be sprayed green if you so desire.

There are always some flowering shrubs that are best preserved as they grew, that is, with both flowers and leaves on the branch, such as the mock orange. These require the sand treatment and also some reinforcing of the color after they are removed from the desiccant. Obviously they cannot be sprayed or the flowers would be ruined, so the only way that I know of is to go over each leaf with a brushing of thin green stain. Do the fronts of all leaves first, then go back and stain the backs. Acrylic paint is very effective in this procedure.

I have compiled two lists of foliage, one of leaves and one of sprays. The lists are composed of greenery which is either indigenous to the area in which I live or specimens that have been sent to me. Other areas would certainly include other varieties. My suggestion is to experiment with the varieties that are available to you, trying both methods and then deciding for yourself which is best.

## LEAVES

| TYPE | METHOD | TIME | SPECIAL TREATMENT |
|------|--------|------|-------------------|
| *Achillea* | sand | 2 weeks | Spray after drying |
| *Ajuga* | glycerin | until done | Optional spraying |

‡‡ 103 ‡‡

# Ways to Preserve Foliage

| TYPE | METHOD | TIME | SPECIAL TREATMENT |
|------|--------|------|-------------------|
| *Althaea* | sand or glycerin | until done | Optional spraying |
| *Anemone* | sand | 2 weeks | Spray after drying |
| *Artemesia* | sand | 2 weeks | Spray after drying |
| *Astilbe* | sand | 2 weeks | Spray after drying |
| *Beech* | glycerin | until done | Optional spraying |
| *Begonia* | sand | 2 weeks | Optional spraying |
| *Bleeding heart* | sand | 2 weeks | Spray after drying |
| *Butterfly bush* | sand | 2 weeks | Spray after drying |
| *Caladium* | sand | 3 weeks | Do not spray |
| *Camellia* | glycerin | until done | Optional spraying |
| *Canna* | sand or glycerin | until done | Optional spraying |
| *Castor bean* | sand | 2 weeks | Spray after drying |
| *Catalpa* | sand | 2 weeks | Spray after drying |
| *Coleus* | sand | 2 weeks | Do not spray |
| *Columbine* | sand | 2 weeks | Spray after drying |
| *Coral bells* | sand | 2 weeks | Spray after drying |
| *Corydalis brandegei* | sand | 2 weeks | Spray after drying |
| *Croton* | sand | 3 weeks | Do not spray |
| *Delphinium* | sand | 2 weeks | Spray after drying |
| *Dusty miller* | air dry | until firm | Do not spray |
| *Ferns* | sand | 2 weeks | Spray after drying |
| *Feverfew* | sand | 2 weeks | Spray after drying |
| *Fruit leaves* | sand or glycerin | until done | Optional spraying |
| *Funkia* | sand | 2 weeks | Do not spray |
| *Golden rain* | glycerin | until done | Optional spraying |
| *Grape* | sand | 2 weeks | Spray after drying |
| *Honey locust* | glycerin | until done | Spray after drying |
| *Hydrangea* | sand | 2 weeks | Spray after drying |
| *Iris* | sand or glycerin | until done | Optional spraying |
| *Jacaranda* | sand | 2 weeks | Spray after drying |
| *Lamb's ears* | air dry | until firm | Do not spray |
| *Laurel* | glycerin | until done | Optional spraying |
| *Leather fern* | glycerin | until done | Optional spraying |
| *Leatherleaf* | sand | 2 weeks | Spray after drying |
| *Lemon* | glycerin | until done | Optional spraying |
| *Lily of the valley* | sand | 2 weeks | Spray after drying |
| *Lupine* | sand | 2 weeks | Spray after drying |
| *Magnolia* | glycerin | until done | Optional spraying |
| *Maidenhair fern* | sand | 2 weeks | Spray after drying |
| *Marguerite* | sand | 2 weeks | Spray after drying |

## Ways to Preserve Foliage

| TYPE | METHOD | TIME | SPECIAL TREATMENT |
|------|--------|------|-------------------|
| *Mountain ash* | sand or glycerin | until done | Spray after drying |
| *Oak* | glycerin | until done | Optional spraying |
| *Oregon grape* | sand | 2 weeks | Spray after drying |
| *Palm* | sand | 2 weeks | Optional spraying |
| *Papyrus* | sand | 2 weeks | Spray after drying |
| *Peony* | glycerin | until done | Spray after drying |
| *Ranunculus* | sand | 2 weeks | Spray after drying |
| *Rhododendron* | glycerin | until done | Optional spraying |
| *Snowball* | sand | 2 weeks | Spray after drying |
| *Snow-on-the-mountain* | sand | 2 weeks | Do not spray |
| *Thalictrum* | sand | 2 weeks | Spray after drying |
| *Violet* | sand | 2 weeks | Spray after drying |
| *Water lily* | sand | 2 weeks | Spray after drying |
| *Yarrow* | sand | 2 weeks | Spray after drying |
| *Yucca* | sand | 4 weeks | Spray after drying |

## SPRAYS

| TYPE | METHOD | TIME | SPECIAL TREATMENT |
|------|--------|------|-------------------|
| *Azalea* | sand | 2 weeks | Paint leaves with a brush after drying |
| *Bridal wreath* | sand | 2 weeks | Use as is—impossible to spray or paint |
| *Broom* | air dry | until firm | Optional spraying |
| *Camellia* | glycerin | until done | Optional spraying |
| *Choke cherry* | sand | 2 weeks | May be painted after drying |
| *Christmas greens:* | | | |
|   *Balsam* | | | |
|   *Cedar* | | | |
|   *Fir* | | | |
|   *Juniper* | | | |
|   *Pine* | | | |
|   *Spruce* | | | |
|   *Yew* | glycerin | until done | Spray after drying |
| *Chrysanthemum* | sand | 2 weeks | Spray after drying |
| *Clematis* | sand | 2 weeks | Spray after drying |
| *Cotoneaster* | glycerin | until done | Optional spraying |
| *Creeping Jenny* | sand or glycerin | until done | Spray after drying |
| *Eglantine* | sand | 2 weeks | Spray after drying |

# Ways to Preserve Foliage

| TYPE | METHOD | TIME | SPECIAL TREATME… |
|------|--------|------|------------------|
| *Euonymus* | glycerin | until done | Spray after dryin… |
| *Fuchsia* | sand | 2 weeks | Spray after dryin… |
| *Hawthorn* | sand | 2 weeks | Spray after dryin… if no flowers on s… |
| *Hemlock* | glycerin | until done | Spray after dryin… |
| *Holly* | glycerin | until done | Spray after dryin… |
| *Ivy* | sand or glycerin | until done | Spray after dryin… |
| *Japanese quince* | sand | 2 weeks | If no flowers, spr… if flowers on, spr… paint |
| *Lemon* | glycerin | until done | Optional spraying… |
| *Lilac* | sand | 2 weeks | Spray after dryin… |
| *Lily* | sand | 2 weeks | Spray after dryin… |
| *Magnolia* | glycerin | until done | Optional spraying… |
| *Maple* | warm iron | ironing time | Do not spray |
| *Matrimony vine* | sand | 2 weeks | Spray after dryin… |
| *Mock orange* | sand | 2 weeks | Paint both sides o… leaves after dryin… |
| *Mosses* | air dry | few days | Dip in green liqui… dye after drying |
| *Myrtle* | glycerin or sand | until done | Spray after dryin… |
| *Rosa hugonis* | sand | 2 weeks | Spray after dryin… |
| *Roses* | sand or glycerin | until done | Spray after dryin… |
| *Smilax* | sand | 2 weeks | Spray after dryin… |
| *Snowball* | sand | 2 weeks | Spray after dryin… |
| *Spiraea* | sand | 2 weeks | Spray after dryin… |
| *Tamarisk* | air dry | 1 week | Do not spray |
| *Thalictrum* | sand | 2 weeks | Spray after dryin… |
| *Wandering Jew* | sand | 2 weeks | Optional spraying… |
| *Weeping trees* | sand or glycerin | until done | Optional spraying… |

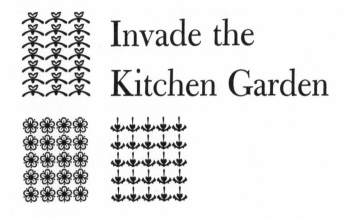

# CHAPTER XIII

# Invade the
# Kitchen Garden

Yes, invade the kitchen garden and see what lovely treasures await your preserving arts. Strawberries, bush fruits, grapes, herbs and vegetables all are grown to delight the palate and nourish the body, yet each has something to offer by way of decoration.

Vegetable and fruit gardens are with us year after year, but herb gardens, as such, seem to have been relegated to the past. What a pity! There was a time when they were of paramount importance not only for their beauty but as a source of medicine, flavoring for foods, perfuming and dyeing of materials. There is a growing tendency to revive some of their importance in kitchen gardens today. If you are fortunate enough to have herbs growing in your garden, they will provide some priceless treasures for preservation.

Too often we tend to ignore these lowly subjects, both vegetable and herb, without thinking of their decorative values. We tear off a wealth of ferny greens from a carrot, discard it as waste, when its delicate tracery could add charm to many a bouquet. The tomato leaf has such interest and form that its equal is seldom found among the garden flowers. I repeat, invade the kitchen garden with an unprejudiced eye for beauty and see what new discoveries you can make.

The potato is another challenging subject for consideration. Few plants have more attractive leaves. They are of a deep rich green, heavily veined, with a graceful indented contour; characteristics that make them ideal for an accompaniment to flowers.

Its blossoms, though small, are of exquisite form and coloring, and when dried and grouped together, they give an appearance of a cluster of shooting stars or miniature cyclamen in purple and white.

I have previously mentioned the foliage of the tomato and carrot as being worthy of preservation, but there is another in the same category that we cannot afford to ignore—parsley. We can never get enough of fern-like foliage for our arrangements and this is, indeed, another fern-like addition. Best of all, when it is skillfully arranged with flowers, no one will ever guess what it is. Even if they did, they would compliment you on your imagination and thrift.

Corn tassels and ornamental corn can be used as an appropriate and refreshing accent in fall decorations. The tassels are already dry by the time the corn has ripened so they will need no more preparation unless your imagination takes wings and you decide to dip them in liquid dye of your choice. I visualize them tinted in many of the wood tones of autumn. They would thus produce a striking effect when combined with other fall materials such as ornamental corn and gourds.

Pumpkin flowers are beautiful subjects in both form and color. How many people have really ever looked closely at them? When separated from the vine and displayed singly, they resemble an exotic Oriental bloom. No wonder the Orientals use them to decorate their foods, and for that matter, even eat them upon occasion. Try drying some.

Ornamental kale or cabbages need no introduction. Many flower catalogues list them along with choice flowers. They come in red, white and green, and a combination of red on green. I have even seen some in the pink and lavender shades. I have seen magnificent specimens of them displayed singly, along with flowers, and they always proved to be the conversation pieces of the exhibit. I have never tried to dry cabbages because I have never been able to grow them. But I have always hoped that some adventurous flower dryer would try them some day. The complete head could be dried as a unit because there would be no danger of its falling apart in the sand and the leaves are substantial enough to hold their upright shape in the sand while the head is being covered. I would suggest that a very long time be allowed for drying, perhaps as much as two months. I would make sure that a thin filling of sand was sprinkled between each leaf and some additional heat would help to speed up the drying. If you succeeded, it would be well worth the effort. If not, you could try single leaves and use them in an arrangement with other dried material.

Lovage and borage are two plants that should not be ignored. They are classed as herbs. The pale blue flowers of the borage plant were formerly used to decorate foods and were also candied for a sweet. When dusted with blue powdered chalk and dried, they help fill the need for blue in arrangements. Lovage has long glossy dark green leaves that are hard to beat in the foliage world and are easily preserved in sand.

The term "lavender" always reminds me of English cottage gardens, although it is grown extensively in most of the Mediterranean countries for its exquisite perfume. The long spikes of lavender dry well, although they take on a darker shade. They also have the right to be included in a Victorian arrangement, and, in addition, they will impart a lingering fragrance to the bouquet as long as it lasts.

Sage contributes an exotic blue spiked flower in early summer that turns a purple-blue when dried. It, too, lends a spicy aroma to the mixed bouquet.

There is also the strawberry bed whose single white flowers with yellow centers resemble tiny single white roses. The plant from which they bloom also produces long vines, called runners. A strawberry vine is decorative indeed when used to decorate a bowl of fresh fruit.

Several years ago I dried a collection of such vines by burying them in sand. All along the central stem or vine are leaves of graduated sizes, starting from the base with fully grown ones, then gradually getting smaller as they reached the tip of the vine. The flowers were cut off and dried individually. Then I fitted a small, flat, wicker basket with the strawberry fruits when they were ripe and twined the vines up and around the handle and down among the berries. I put the white dried flowers back on the vines at intervals with a bit of glue. The finished product was delightful to look at and appetizing to eat. A permanent arrangement such as this could be made by following the directions in a subsequent chapter in the book entitled "Flower Sculpture."

While speaking of fruit blossoms, let me remind you to preserve some complete clusters (leaves and flowers) to be used as garnishments for bowls of fruit. They will add a fresh touch and added interest to the most commonplace collection of fruit found in nearly every home the year around.

If you are fortunate enough to live in an area where artichokes grow, plant some; let them grow and bloom and then reap a truly golden harvest. You can buy the artichokes to eat in almost every grocery store but you cannot buy the blossoms. I have never been fortunate enough to even see them growing, but some of the most striking arrangements I have ever seen have been made with artichoke blooms that had been dipped in liquid dye and allowed to dry. All colors are beautiful, but I believe my favorites were the huge fluffy, ball-shaped blossoms that were dyed a soft sage green; they were truly a decorator's delight.

Perhaps of all of the kitchen garden inhabitants, none is more useful than the chive. The story of the chive was included in my first book. It proved to be very popular with my readers; so, by request, I am also including it in the present edition. I call it the "million dollar plant."

## The Story of the Chive

As I have often stated, too many people think that flower drying consists of applying some magic formula to a flower that will cause it to be forever preserved in all its original perfection and glory. Unfortunately a great deal of knowledge and technique must usually go into the process. There is, however, one plant whose performance does indeed seem magical. This is the Allium schoenoprasum, or just plain chives to you and me.

You can buy chives at a nursery, but many grocery stores sell them too. A clump will cost you about fifty cents, or you may purchase a packet of seeds for around thirty cents. The seeds sprout quickly and one packet should give you at least a hundred plants. Since they are perennials, they will reproduce profusely year after year. Yet they are the humble folk of the plant world, asking little, yet giving much. A diet of rather poor soil satisfies them and they need little water, but like most of God's children, they do want their "place in the sun."

Chives are listed as herbs and are grown mainly as seasoning for foods. Although they belong to the onion family, they have achieved a refinement and delicacy that their more earthy cousin lacks. An entire cookbook could and should be written about their many virtues in the sauce pot.

You may revel in the lift they give to mundane foods. Cut them as close to the ground as you wish, and almost before you have ceased smacking your lips over the last *pièce de résistance*, they are up again and ready for another cutting. You can keep this up for the entire growing season or even the whole year, depending upon the climate in which you live.

But, here's the best part: the chive has a flower. Every spring myriads of tough, straight stems appear, each topped with a minute bud. Continue to cut the green tops as often as you wish, but let these flower stems grow and bloom. Soon you will be delighted by what looks like a bed of amethysts sparkling in your garden. Each flower head, which measures from one to two inches in diameter, consists of dozens of tiny, bell-shaped florets grouped closely together and resembling a fluffy ball. Cut each flower stem as close to the ground as you can. You will need as long a stem as you can get.

Now make your flower arrangement, and that's all. Chives need no drying medium; they need not even be hung upside down. And the flowers won't shrink, wither, or change color. In short, your arrangement of fresh chives will preserve itself permanently.

You may not want lavender in your bouquet. If you require fall tones or some other color combination, chives will give it to you. You may dip them in flower dye of any shade or tint and they will take it beautifully. You may even concoct colors and hues of your own by dipping them in one color and then in another, or even in a third, to produce beautifully muted tones rarely seen in nature but which lend themselves so well to the art of decoration. If you err and get a color too dark for your purposes, swish the flowers in a pan of cold water. This will remove the excess dye and lighten the flowers to the desired shade.

But we are not through yet with this floral manna. If, by chance, you haven't the time to dye the chives while they are fresh, stand them upright in an empty can (no water please) and dye them at your leisure after they have become dry. Thus you will have more time to enjoy the fun of the dyeing process. They will respond just as well to your whims now as when they are freshly cut, even to the swishing in cold water. They will remain as steadfast and straight as little soldiers during and after this ordeal. Neither humidity nor heat nor cold will have the slightest effect on their good behavior, either now or in the months to come.

Since chives lend themselves beautifully to miniature arrangements, the containers should be small. I choose porcelain egg cups which are available at most chain and dime stores. To prepare the containers, fill a salt shaker with fine sand or table salt. Next, paint the outside surface of the cup with water-thinned mucilage, plain varnish, or clear floral spray. While the surface is still wet, sprinkle it with salt or fine sand and allow it to dry thoroughly. Then paint both the inside and the outside of the cup with gold, silver or copper metallic paint, available at most paint and hobby stores. To mix, follow the directions on the package. The metallic paint gives a charming, nugget-like setting for your jewels. But you can paint the cups with other colors or simply leave them white.

Bits of dried greenery tucked in here and there among the flowers add to the effect. The greens can be pressed between pages of books and because they are very small, their flatness will go unnoticed. A sprig or two of baby's breath (which also dries by itself), either white or dyed, will add a touch of airiness to the arrangement. One final note: If you wish, you can glue a tiny white butterfly to a flower head.

You needn't be a gardener to enjoy chives; they can be grown by anyone. Here is an intriguing way to teach children the art of growing things and creating beauty. The procedures are simple enough for any small child. A pot of chives in any sunny window can be a boon to apartment dwellers who have no opportunity to satisfy a desire to dig in the soil and grow things. Consider the therapeutic value that growing these plants could have for semi-invalids or for those suffering from nervous strain. It could create a new interest for people too old to engage in the strenuous care of a garden.

Here, too, is a delightful way to say "Merry Christmas" or "Happy Birthday" to your friends and loved ones, or to bring cheer to a patient in a hospital. The giving of this little plant is without equal in the world.

# CHAPTER XIV

# Wild Material

It has been said that there are about 50,000 different kinds of flowering plants in the United States. I do not know whether they are native or not. I doubt it. For instance the cactus is found in many countries throughout the world. Every section of the country has its own particular varieties which are dependent upon climatic conditions, rainfall, and soil content, although there are some kinds that seem to thrive almost everywhere. Whether you live in the mountains, near the seashore, in swamp areas, or on the desert, you will find some particular types of wild flowers growing there. But in order to find them you have to look for them.

### Uses for Wild Plants

The search for and collecting of wild material is a MUST for the botany student. Here the old adage that one look is worth a thousand words proves to be true. Armed with his technical knowledge, he must see for himself nature's application of these formulated rules in the living plant.

For prolonged observation and comparative study the plant should be preserved. Of what use is a bunch of drooping, wilted material to a botany class? Pressed flowers are not the answer, either, because here the material is flattened—artificially distorted into two dimensions only. Clearly, flower preservation is not only the solution but a necessity, if the student is to be able to study the living plant in all of its growth habits, from the root formation on through to the topmost bud. A large part of my correspondence has come from botany students who were interested in learning this art. Many of them have taken up flower preservation as their class project.

The interest in this art need not be confined to the botany student. He should work hand in hand with the chemistry department. The subtle and even abrupt changes in color, texture and sometimes contour in the preserved specimen, should be of direct interest to the chemist, particularly if any advancement is to be made in the art of flower preservation itself. One of my greatest regrets is that I have not a full lifetime to devote to these two subjects. One who does, with flower preservation in mind, is bound to come up with some startling discoveries that would become a lasting contribution to the flower world.

The importance of a collection of wild plant material for a museum of natural history is self-evident, particularly if the material is indigenous to that particular area. Again, the only satisfactory way to accomplish this is through flower preservation. Far too many of our National Parks and museums exhibit only pressed specimens and these always lack the feeling of the growing plant.

Several years ago I preserved forty-five specimens of flowering plants in their entirety for the United States Forest Service. The collection included plants that bloomed from early spring to late fall. They were displayed in the Visitor's Center at Red Canyon, Utah. There thousands of people have seen and enjoyed them and, indeed, there is no other way by which the tourist could visualize the actual plant life of that area. The same thing could and should be done in every area. Collections of stuffed animals, birds, and even geological specimens are usually exhibited there, why not a representation of preserved native plants?

Of course I am not overlooking the collecting and preservation of wild flowers for your very own pleasure. This, in itself, is a worthwhile project. There are some people who prefer wild flowers to any cultivated kinds. I am one of them because my favorite flower is the desert cactus. Then there is the wild rose which lends itself so beautifully to decoration.

You may even wish to start a wild flower garden of your own. If there is a part of your garden that answers their needs it can be done, either by seeds or plants. Your library will supply garden books' that give the necessary instructions for their planting and care. A fine one is Senator Aiken's *Pioneering with Wildflowers*. Perhaps the greatest pleasure of all to be gained from any of these projects will be the increased knowledge and enjoyment of the treasures of the great outdoors.

### Rules to Follow

Whatever your purpose is, there are a few preliminary rules to follow before you begin. Do not attempt to preserve wild flowers until you have mastered the techniques of the art. Here the time element is of great importance. The specimen must be prepared and processed with speed before wilting takes place. Once the material is on hand and waiting, there is not time for references, experiment, or fumbling with materials. This necessary preliminary experience comes through doing cultivated ones first. The problems of wild flowers are many and they require fast, accurate judgment and work. Unlike the tame pets, they have their wild eccentricities and you will figuratively need a whip and a chair to bring some of them into subjugation. However, we will meet these special problems when we are confronted with them.

Make sure you get the necessary permission to gather your wild material. Even if the flowers grow on a vacant lot, you may avoid possible trouble by first getting the landowner's permission to remove them. If your project is of a scientific nature or a community gift, a letter or call to your local Forest Service Center will no doubt give you the permission and assistance you require. The Wild Flower Preservation Society, 3740 Oliver St., Washington, D.C. 20015, has lists of plants which should be protected in different sections of the country. It will cooperate with individuals or groups who wish to preserve the growing of wild flowers and undoubtedly will give you valuable advice on obtaining the kinds you wish to acquire.

Observe the cutting laws. Keep in mind that making a collection does not permit anyone to violate state laws protecting wild flowers. Always make sure that there is more than one specimen growing in the area before you cut it. If there are others of the same kind nearby, they will reseed themselves or increase by underground bulbs and stems. Unless you have need for a scientific study of the root system of transplanting, do not uproot the plant. Leave plenty of stem aboveground when cutting. Unless these laws are carefully observed our wild flower population will soon disappear, particularly since such tremendous inroads have been made in our wild areas in the name of civilization.

I live near a government reserve property. Until recently it was completely fenced in and no trespassing was allowed. The fields in their natural state were profuse with sego lilies, the state flower, and the law forbids their cutting or removal. Several years ago a portion of the land was acquired for a private housing project. Imagine the pain we experienced upon seeing the great bulldozers plow up the land, thus destroying acres of these precious flowers. With a bit of foresight, permission could have been granted to flower lovers to dig them up and transplant them to their own gardens or other areas. So even our government officials don't always cooperate in observing the laws they are supposed to enforce.

The wonderful world of cactus is fast disappearing in our arid Southwest as the ever increasing cultivation creeps in. So goes our wild life. Some species have disappeared completely, much to our common loss. So again my admonition is, cut with care and consideration, so that generations to come will not be robbed of their rightful heritage, the pleasure of walking among fields of wild flowers.

Get to know your regional plants—their names, characteristics, where to find them. If you learn the names of their different parts, pistil, stamens, sepals, petals, spurs, etc., it will help you in identifying them. Flowers are also classified as ray, irregular, composite, and disc flowers. There are many good regional wild flower books that are available. A request to the National Park Service should supply the needed information.

## Wild Material

Your local library or bookstore can supply you with many. Your pleasure in collecting wild flowers will be doubled if you can identify them.

## Materials Needed

Assemble all the materials you will need before you start out on your wild flower expedition. Nothing is as frustrating as to come upon a clump of special beauties and find that you don't have the proper knife or shears to sever them. You usually end up by trying to break them off, either ruining the plant or the flowers or both.

Appropriate clothing is important no matter where you are going. If it is in the mountains, you may need warm clothing; in the desert, the reverse. But wherever it is you should be properly clothed. The dangers of thorns, poisonous weeds and insects is lessened if the body is completely covered. Shoes are of special importance. They should be low-heeled, fairly heavy and comfortable. Remember I said shoes—not open sandals. Always include a pair of work gloves. Some plants are irritating to the skin and you never know when a sturdy glove will help prevent a bleeding knuckle. A good pair of sunglasses may prove helpful. If the day is windy take along a sweater and scarf. This list should take care of your physical comforts.

Your plant equipment is more precise. A large pair of cutting shears is a must, also a strong cutting knife. If you are going to the desert, by all means include a pair of tongs for handling prickly material. If you do not you will be sorry because the heaviest leather gloves will not be sufficient to protect you against the barbs of the cactus. You will also need several containers of water or a keeping solution. Do not put your trust in finding water there—take it with you.

In Chapter VII, I described the formula for a very good keeping solution that one of my pupils gave me. I find it particularly useful to carry along on my field expeditions as it keeps the flowers fresh longer than just plain water. The cut material should be put in the container of solution immediately after cutting. Protect all cut material from strong winds and direct sunlight. Do not cut more than you can preserve at one time, because even with the best of care, wild material will not keep more than a short period of time.

Carry a notebook and pencil with you and write down the location, date, and types of flowers growing in a given location. This information will be of use to you in future years if you wish to make a return trip. All of these materials should be put in a cardboard carton for convenience and the carton, itself, may come in handy for other dry materials you may come across on your trip. It is certainly a must if your search is for cactus.

Keep a weather eye out for interesting bunches of seed pods, acorns, berries, pine cones, bark, lichens, grasses, interesting branches and weathered wood. If the trip is near a stream, mosses and cattails may be found; if it is near the ocean, look for interesting shells. These are all of an everlasting quality and have no need for further treatment, other than grooming or an occasional coat of shellac, unless a dye bath or a metallic spray of some other color would suit your decorating whim.

## Techniques of Preserving

All wild plants, both flowers and foliage, must be processed in sand or other dry desiccant. They should not be subjected to the glycerin method. The few exceptions to this rule would be the heavy-textured foliage which is intended for decorative purposes only. I treat the mountain boxwood in this manner.

The covering and uncovering of the plant is done exactly as you did the cultivated ones; either face up, face down or horizontal. Your common sense and experience will dictate the method.

It may be that you wish to reinforce the color of the flowers before processing. This may be done with a small camel's hair brush, using the selfsame color of powdered chalk. Use care not to overlap the color on stamens and foliage. The coloring should be done while the stems of the plant are still in the container of water and before you cut off the flowers. These are delicate creatures and need all the liquid sustenance they can get in order to survive the shock of cutting.

*Wild Material*

If the plant is to be done in its entirety a different problem presents itself. Parts of the plant that you would ordinarily discard as worthless in garden flowers must be included. Indeed, every branch, leaf, blossom, bud, seed pod, spent blossom and often the root system must receive special care if the plant is to be used for scientific purposes.

Cut the flowers, one at a time, and process each before proceeding to the next one. Buds that show color should be done in the same way. Leave enough stem on them to hold the glue when you replace them, which you must do after they are dried.

If the plant is too large and cumbersome to do as a single unit, cut it into convenient sections, starting with one side branch or the top as the case may be. Make sure that a pin is inserted in the end of the cut section and also at the point of severance from the central stem. It would be well to number these sections before processing by slipping a small piece of paper with a number written on it through the pin, before it is inserted in the cut end. The number on the severed branch should correspond to the number on the pin inserted in the central stem. This is done to facilitate the assembling of the plant in its original form after it is dried. Process one branch or section before cutting the next one, and proceed downward toward the root.

If the root system is to be included in the finished specimen, the plant should be carefully dug and carried home encased in its surrounding soil. Once home, the soil must be carefully washed out and the entire root system placed immediately in a large container of water. As you proceed with the cutting and covering, leave a portion of the central stem attached to the root system for easier assembling. Carefully dry the last section, the root system, with an absorbent cloth, number both cut ends and process with the same care for maintaining its original contour that you would use for any other section. Thus you may preserve a plant in its entirety no matter what its size or dimensions are.

The flowers of such plants are usually quite large or grow in clusters. Unless they are first removed and processed individually, the proper attention cannot be given them and the branch at the same time. They would be crushed and distorted while covering the branch. Each unit demands your full attention and care. If the stems of the flowers are thick enough to permit the insertion of a pin, they can be put back in place with ease after the plant is completed. If not, they must be glued back on. Some examples would be: the wild hollyhock, choke cherry, wild rose, clematis, etc.

Do not remove the flowers if the plant is of a spiked variety whose florets are clustered close to the central stem, and which can be processed as a single unit. The position they would assume in the sand would be determined by the position the individual flowers assume on the stem. If the bells or florets point downward, do them face down in order to fill the centers with sand; if upward or outward, use the face-up or horizontal position. Such examples would include the gilia, pentstemon, delphinium, and so forth.

The uncovering of wild material is the same as for the cultivated varieties, but the aftertreatment may present some unforeseen problems. In any case, it is advisable to clean each specimen immediately upon removal from the desiccant before uncovering the next one. The entire plant is more flexible at this time and less subject to breakage during the cleaning process.

One of the problems that you may encounter is the unusually heavy coating of desiccant adhering to the stems and leaves of certain wild material. This is due to the excess of sticky substance with which nature endowed the plant for the purpose of attracting insects. This sticky substance dries as the plant is being desiccated, and of course all of the grains that come in contact with it are attached firmly to the leaf, as if they were glued there. In this case, the usual brushing process is useless. I solved this problem in the following way: select a very large plastic bag. Put some water in it and swish it all around in the bag. Then empty all of the water out, leaving only the beads of moisture that adhere to the bag naturally. Lay the bag on a smooth flat surface. Prop the bag open in the center with several coat hangers, allowing the long straight ends to rest on the bottom of the bag, and the hook-ends to support the top.

Now fold a soft towel and lay it through the coat hangers, forming a cushion on the bottom of the bag. Place the foliage on the towel, making sure no part of it touches the damp, plastic bag. Crush the open ends of the bag together and fasten with an elastic band. Allow the foliage to remain, thus enclosed, for several hours, or until they have absorbed enough of the moisture inside to soften up their textures. Remove them one at a time and brush carefully. You will find that the sand has become loosened and the leaf can be cleaned with ease with no danger of breakage.

As I have stated elsewhere in this book, wild material intended for botanical or scientific study should be preserved, cleaned, assembled and presented for study without any touching up or application of other additives, the only exception being the application of a moisture-proofing spray if the humidity is so dense that there is danger of the plant collapsing.

There is a way to test the plant before this happens. Gently touch the leaves and flowers. If all rigidity has left them and they feel soft and pliable to the touch, they have probably reached their peak of endurance. They should be moved into a warm room, such as a kitchen, with the oven on and the doors closed, and allowed to dry out for several hours. Then spray according to directions.

There are some plants which require a moisture-proofing spray no matter where you live. One is the evening primrose. I have preserved this beautiful plant only to have the blossoms collapse after several months, and I live in a very dry climate. Another flowering plant is the creeping phlox that grows so profusely on the dry mountain hillsides in the spring. I revived the pink petals twice by ironing them individually over my finger, one at a time; a nerve-wracking experience, especially if the iron got a bit too hot. But eventually they curled up again. The next time I do them they will be given a thorough spraying right from the start. And if that fails they will be given a coating of Flower Sculpture Formula, on the underside of the petals only.

Dried material meant to last for an indefinite number of years, such as a museum collection, should definitely have its colors reinforced. Unless this is done, the shapes will remain but the colors will vanish. I advise either painting the foliage or spraying it with a foliage spray as nearly like the original color as possible. If the plant is of an intricate fern-like structure, spraying is advisable before the flowers are replaced. If the specimen was dried with the flowers on, then of course, the greenery must be painted by hand.

Use care and good judgment in the selection of the flowers whose colors you attempt to reinforce. Never apply a dye of any kind to a flower whose silky texture would be altered, such as the cactus. It is better to have it eventually fade than to ruin its chief charm—its luster. The wild rose is another that remains perfect by itself without any further makeup. But always reinforce such coarse-textured flower heads as the Indian paintbrush. Its color will be enhanced and brightened and it will be easier to clean. White flowers remain white longer if given a coating of white powdered chalk.

The most intriguing flower that I know in all the wild kingdom is the cactus. Its story is an epic as it is one of the oldest flowers in existence. It has an unbroken chain of reappearance from the earliest dawn of creation until the present day. Its relatives have invaded the tropics, yet it thrives in the desert. Its story follows, because it is my favorite flower.

### Enduring Beauty of the Cactus Blooms

The prickly pear cactus is known as the gypsy of its clan because it travels everywhere, yet to me it is the aristocrat of all flowers. In the care and preparation it needs for preserving, it breaks every rule in the book.

Cacti do not grow in every backyard, but you can get them. I wanted them so badly I drove eight hundred miles from Salt Lake City to the border of Arizona for them. I carried three hundred pounds or so of sand and about seventy-five containers in the car in order to process them on the spot. After going that distance, I did not intend to take any chances of their withering.

*Wild Material*

It was a long trip and, for the most part, quite a frustrating one as mile after mile rolled by over and around mountains and through sand with no sight of human habitation or cacti. But finally we reached one of Utah's scenic treasures, Monument Valley, which we thought by reason of its very magnificence, should be the home of magnificent flowers. As we pulled into the valley I inquired of an Indian, lounging under a scrub oak and with a face that looked as old as the mountains and valleys, if I could find any cactus thereabouts. He grunted with one of the pleasantest Indian grunts I had ever heard and directed me to a boy, about ten or twelve, just "down the road a piece."

"Sure," the boy said, "just drive up that road until the sand begins to get deep, then park your car or you will get stuck. Then climb the mountain on your left, go down the second ravine past two hogans, and there you'll find them."

So my two companions and I (and you never travel in these areas without companions) did as we were told, plodding through hot sand more than ankle deep. Our eyes never left the ground, which we studied for suspicious-looking holes and slithering tracks in the sand that could mean rattlesnakes. We were packed down with boxes, shears, pliers, knives and other paraphernalia, all of which didn't make walking a delight. And to top it all, a scorching sun was overhead. But at last we reached the spot the Indian boy told us about. And there they were, cacti, a sizable field of them with their satin petals rippling in the noonday sun.

Nature must be very jealous of this delicate child of hers. One cuts and preserves the luscious blooms at the risk of shooting pains and infected fingers. So numerous and so fine and sharp are the barbs that they go right through any clothing and into the flesh. I wore thick leather gloves and the end result was that I had to burn them. After four months I still have marks on my skin from cacti stickers.

Evidently, however, I was not the only seeker after these exotic flowers, for there were masses of tiny black bugs rollicking among the forest of yellow stamens. This meant of course removing these tiny intruders before putting the blooms

‡‡ 124 ‡‡

in sand. It was noon and hot, and the flowers had the knack of folding up prematurely whenever I attempted to work in the shade.

I had deliberately cut a number of complete fleshy pears, intending to reassemble the flowers on the mother plant when they were dry. These I threw in a box and carried home in the car trunk. What a surprise I had after I arrived! For when I opened the trunk I discovered that my cactus had bloomed. Apparently I had cut portions that not only held the flower I had wanted, but contained other buds as well. I laid the cut portions of cactus in full sun on our patio and had a succession of blooms every day for two weeks. Every bud came into full bloom. So I learned my lesson. No longer do I carry drying materials to the cactus—but bring the cactus to them. Nor do I need the full pear to bring forth a bloom; a cut portion is sufficient to bring the bud into flower. Even the tiny bugs disappear; being creatures of the wild, they desert the plants as soon as they are removed from their native home.

The cut pear must be left standing upright or the flower will be lopsided when it opens. This means that some slight bracing must be done. I usually stand them against the sides of a shallow berry box. If you leave the pads there long enough every one will develop a root system without the aid of soil or water. You may then plant them in your garden if you have the dry sunny spot which they demand. All handling of both flower and pad MUST be done with pliers or tongs. NEVER touch any part of this wild creature with your hands. They resent your touch as much as you dread theirs. They don't seem to resent the hordes of insects and bugs that inhabit them in the wilds, but if you as much as touch their stamens, they will curl up in a tight mass. Great care must be taken in cutting them from the mother pad and getting them on the bed of sand without ever touching a single stamen, and all this must be done with pliers—quite a trick.

The covering process involves the following: Have your container ready with about an inch of sand in the bottom. Secure the two handles of a small pair of pliers with an elastic band. Your flower stem is to be held between them and they might separate and you would lose your flower. With the pliers in your left hand, enclose them around the prickly, fleshy stem just under the flower itself. Now with a pair of sharp shears cut the fleshy stem off at the point where it is joined to the pad. Carry the flower (with the pliers) to your containers and push the stem in the sand, face up, being very careful not to touch the stamens. When it is firmly anchored, grasp a small handful of sand and quickly dribble it through the stamens, then another handful if necessary to anchor them in place. Once this is done, you may proceed with the covering of the flower in the usual manner.

Do not leave the cactus flowers in the sand too long. Ten days are long enough. The fleshy stem will not dry completely in that length of time but the flower will and it will have a more beautiful sheen and the petals can be more easily cleaned. Uncover the flower as you would any other, that is letting the blossom fall face forward in your right hand. Remember, pick it up by the stem with the pliers, not with your fingers.

It is well to clean the flower as soon as it emerges from the sand. The petals are delicate and fragile and if the desiccant is allowed to remain on them indefinitely there is danger of distortion. Before you clean them have ready a large shallow box and do all your cleaning over this. The stem must be held with pliers while this is being done. This may seem a bit awkward to you at first, but you will soon get used to it. It must be done this way in order to prevent the barbs that are loosened from lodging in your clothing and hands.

After the flower is cleaned, a wire may be inserted in the end of the soft stem (still holding it with the pliers), wrapped with floral tape and painted green. Touch up the prickly stem with paint as well.

The flowers may be joined to the mother pad if you prefer. This is done by inserting a short section of wire in the pad and then pushing the soft stem of the flower into the wire down to the pad (with pliers). The pad is not processed. I know of no way to accomplish this, so the life of the plant is limited. After about a year the pad will dry and fade; however, new green shoots will still emerge from time to time for an indefinite number of years. Unless you are preparing a specimen for exhibition purpose, I see no need of replacing the flowers on the mother plant, which certainly does not have the beauty to grace a living or dining room. But the blossoms will be spectacular in any setting. As I write this, I am enjoying an exquisite collection of pink ones combined with maidenhair fern and arranged in a Lalique vase. The artistry of this fine crystal is a perfect complement for their shimmering beauty.

The real beauty of the cactus is not fully revealed until the flower is preserved. It definitely improves through drying. What was originally satin now becomes a luminous chiffon. The blossoms last but one day, usually. The yellow ones open in the morning a clear primrose tint, but as the flower ages, the deeper and more brilliant tones appear. About noon the petals close up forever, the petals take on the rich sunset shades. In order to collect a full symphony of colors, the flower must be cut at various times of the day.

If you are a lover of floral beauty, it is worth the time and expense to visit cactus land, no matter where you live. As I said, if you want cacti badly enough, they can be had. However, one word of caution: in some areas of the West cacti are protected. Before collecting any specimens, write the Department of Agriculture at the state capital for information.

The following list of Western wild flowers is made up of those with which I have had experience and can therefore recommend for preservation. Many of them are found in other parts of the country and the botanical families to which they belong are varied enough to permit the student to include and subject other near flower relatives to the same treatment. They are listed alphabetically by their common names for quick recognition. The reader is advised to review the following chapters for clarity of terms, methods and special treatments: "Covering the Flower," "Uncovering and Cleaning the Flower," "How to Prepare Stems," "Ways to Preserve Foliage" and "Flower Sculpture."

*Aster*—Face up; two weeks in sand. Be especially careful when removing flowers from sand as they shatter easily.

Reinforce from center with diluted glue. If necessary, touch up yellow centers with powdered chalk to restore fresh look. Process foliage in usual manner, spray or paint green. When dry apply flowers with dab of glue.

*Balsam* (Hairy Leaf)—Face up; two weeks in sand. Use pins. Brush petals with yellow chalk before processing. When dry, spray for humidity. Even with this treatment the flower tends to droop in damp weather so I give the outside (only) of the petals a coating of the Flower Sculpture Formula, tinted yellow, to fortify the structure of the petals.

The leaves are always covered with a sticky substance which attracts insects, and also attracts the sand which, when dried, is very difficult to remove without breaking the leaves. A generous brushing with baby talcum powder, before processing, will help to correct this tendency somewhat, but even then it may be necessary to subject them to the damp plastic bag treatment, described in the first part of this chapter. When all the sand has been removed, the hairy surface and color may be preserved by brushing the leaf on both sides with the selfsame colored powdered chalk.

*Balsam* (Arrow Leaf)—The flowers are treated in the same way as the Hairy Leaf type above. The foliage presents no particular problem as it is smooth surfaced. Spray or paint the selfsame color of green.

*Balsam* (Big Leaf)—Preservation of the flowers is the same as for the above two. Foliage should be treated in the same way as the Hairy Leaf type.

*Black-eyed Susan*—Face up; two weeks in sand. Use pins, brush both sides of petals with powdered chalk before processing. May be necessary to reinforce petals after drying, with diluted glue. Do this from underside, where rays join purple-brown center. Process foliage in the usual manner. Spray or paint green. When dry apply flowers.

*Wild Material*

*Bluebell* (California)—Brush flowers lightly with colored chalk. Face up; two weeks in sand. Process foliage in usual manner, spray for color and apply flowers with glue.

*Bluebell* (Virginia)—Two weeks in sand. Do not remove flowers from branch. Process in position best suited to permit filling of tiny bells with sand. This will depend on the position individual florets assume. Paint foliage and stems for preservation of color.

*Cacti* (all kinds)—See Story of Cactus, covered in this chapter.

*Catkin*—If only the catkins are needed strip off the other foliage and stand upright in a container to air dry in their natural position. If foliage is required, the entire branch must be given the sand treatment. Use care in permitting the catkins to hang naturally as they are being covered. Allow two weeks in sand. Foliage should be painted. Spray catkins with a clear plastic spray to prevent shattering.

*Cattail*—Gather as soon as mature stage has been reached. Spray with clear plastic spray to prevent shattering. The foliage is dramatic in certain arrangements as well as for museum display and can best be preserved in sand to prevent curling. Allow one month in sand. Spray or paint to restore color.

*Chicory*—Face up; two weeks in sand. The sparse raggedy leaves will dry without the sand treatment. When flowers are dry, apply to stems with glue.

*Choke cherry*—Cut individual flower clusters. Use pins, process either face up or face down two weeks. Process foliage in usual manner. Spray or paint to restore color. Apply flowers when dry.

‡‡ 129 ‡‡

## Wild Material

*Clematis*—Face up; two weeks in sand. Use pins. It is sometimes hard to find but well worth the effort because of its grace and delicate coloring. Cut flowers and process individually. Process the trailing vine in its entirety in a shallow large container, being careful to maintain its natural curves using the horizontal method. Spray or paint before adding flowers.

*Clover*—The red variety is most attractive. Dust flower heads thoroughly with powdered chalk. Use pins. Face up; two weeks in sand. Process stems and leaves in usual manner. They should be hand painted with special care given to white markings on leaves. Apply flowers.

*Columbine*—This beautiful flower is rather difficult to do but worth all the trouble. The hollow spurs contain nectar for the insects. Make sure they are thoroughly coated on the inside with either powdered chalk or baby talcum powder to prevent the collection of hardened sand in the tips. Use pins. Face up; two weeks in sand. Spray for humidity when dry. Process stems and foliage in the usual manner and paint or spray green. Apply flowers.

*Daisy*—The same rules apply to the wild varieties as to the cultivated ones. Use pins. Face up; two weeks in sand. Clean immediately upon removal from sand and gently press yellow centers in place if separation of centers occurs. This is done with small end of toothpick. Spray for moisture and when almost dry, gently apply powdered yellow chalk to centers to restore their color. Process stems and foliage in usual manner, paying special attention to the unusually delicate leaves. Spray green and apply flowers.

*Dandelion*—Dust flowers with yellow chalk. Face-up; two weeks in sand. Process leaves, spray green and reassemble with flowers.

*Delphinium*—Process the entire bloom spike either face up or face down, depending on the direction the florets point; two weeks in sand. Process foliage, spray green and reassemble. There is no need for pins, chalk or moisture-proofing spray here. The preserved specimen will give a good account of itself without these additives.

*Dock*—Cut the plant the desired length at the stage of color—which ranges from green to rich golden brown —you desire. Stand upright to dry. It requires nothing other than a clear plastic spray to prevent shattering.

*Dogtooth violet*—Dust flowers thoroughly with powdered chalk, both inside and outside of petals. Process each violet in its entirety with full length of stem attached. Study the flower before choosing one of the positions it is to assume in covering. The object is to preserve its contour without distortion of petals or stamens and at the same time keep the graceful curve of the stem. Face up may be suggested for one flower, whereas the horizontal method would be better for others. Allow three weeks for processing. Spray for humidity. Process leaves in usual manner. Do not use acrylic paint on leaves as it tends to break down their structure for some unknown reason. Paint with oils.

*Evening primrose*—This interesting plant is fun to watch. Buds that show color will unfold in the evening before your eyes, pop into full bloom and sepals bend downward within a period of minutes. They have provided entertainment for many an evening party that I have given. Dust with chalk. Use pins. Face up; three weeks. They emerge from sand in semi-transparent form so it may be necessary to give them a second dusting with chalk. Spray for humidity. Process foliage in usual manner. Spray green and attach flowers.

*False Solomon's-seal*—Cut the tiny cluster of white flowers at the tip of the branch and dry separately. Use pins. Face-up; two weeks. Use horizontal method for remaining part of plant. Spray or paint green and reassemble.

*Wild Material*

*Fireweed*—Another example of doing the flower stalk in its entirety, or if very tall, cut it in sections and process each section separately. Use pins or portions of toothpick in cut ends for easy assembling after it is dried. Face up; two weeks. Spray for humidity. Large leaves adhering to main stem should be cut off, pinned, dried separately and applied to main stem later. Spray or paint green and assemble flower stalk.

*Forget-me-not*—Unfortunately most wild ones are of a very light color. They can be preserved in this natural state or the color can be enhanced by shaking the flower heads slightly in a bag of darker blue powdered chalk. I chalk mine. Use pins. Face up; two weeks. When dry, I like to restore the tiny yellow eye in each floret by dipping the small end of a toothpick in yellow oil paint that has been thinned slightly with turpentine. Also, every tiny speck of stem must be painted green to remove the chalk stains before assembling on the stems. Process remaining stems and accompanying foliage in the usual manner and spray or paint green, but it must be the same green color used on the flower heads.

*Gentian* (fringed)—Here is a true beauty of the wilds but difficult to find. Use pins. Brush with powdered chalk. Face up; two weeks. Stems and foliage done in usual manner. Spray or paint and reassemble. A true aristocrat when it is finished.

*Geranium*—A marked change in color takes place in the flower after it is dried. I do not advise chalking because this tends to cover up the exquisite veinings and markings on the petals. Face-up; two weeks. Spray for humidity. The foliage is lovely and requires more care in its preservation than the small flower. It may be advisable to sever the larger leaves from the plant, using pins and dry separately. Spray or paint green and reassemble plant.

*Gilia*—This is a difficult one to do. A good specimen is literally covered with tiny scarlet trumpets that are star shaped at their ends. They dry perfectly but the flowers turn somewhat darker than is desirable. To overcome this, each trumpet must be brushed with red powdered chalk, which is quite time consuming, but the result is worth it. Cut off one branch or lateral at a time, place cut end in a container with just enough water to keep it from wilting. Now brush each individual floret with chalk. Use pins in cut ends. Two weeks in the position best suited to fill the florets with sand. This will be determined by the direction taken by the majority of the trumpets. If you object to the chalky look when dried, a quick and light spraying with moisture-proofing spray will remove this look but the flowers will still retain the rich red stain left by the chalk. Process stems and foliage and paint or spray green. Paint every bit of green on the flower heads before assembling.

*Globe mallow*—I have been trying for eighteen years to preserve this lovely plant without success. No matter what process I used, the flowers turned brown and transparent. This summer I succeeded for the first time and three lovely sprays of this plant are now in place with my collection at Red Canyon. This is how I did it. Cut all full and half-blown flowers, along with the buds that show color, as closely as possible to the central stem. Face-up in the sand for two weeks. When dry, mix up a small batch of Flower Sculpture Formula, tinted a coral-orange. Brush on a coating on the backs (only) of the flowers. Place them face down on wax paper and allow them to remain until dry, which should take several days. Now turn them over and coat the insides of the petals of each flower. Allow them to remain on their backs or sides until dry. Process the entire stem with the adhering buds and leaves left on it in sand. When it is dry, paint all green parts and glue on the flowers. The result is entrancing.

*Goldenrod*—If the flowers are to be used in arrangements, the most satisfactory results are obtained by using the hang and dry method. Cut some sprays while the flower buds are still green, others just before the flower opens, others in full bloom. They will dry in a week. Spray all but the full-blown with moisture-proofing spray. When dry, sift colored chalk over them several times, green on green, yellow on yellow. Now spray all of them with a clear plastic spray to prevent shattering. The full-blown ones, if left hanging, will literally explode, forming a small round ball, which resembles acacia. They can now be given the above treatment. The stems must be painted to remove all traces of chalk.

If the plant in its entirety is to be used for scientific study or museum display, it must be given the sand treatment, because of the many tiny leaves adhering to the stem which curl up if left to hang and dry. But the flower heads can be cut off while fresh, chalked or dipped in liquid dye, pins inserted and dried separately from the stem. Face-up in sand for ten days. When dry and cleaned, the flower heads must be sprayed with the clear plastic spray to prevent shattering, dusted with yellow chalk and then sprayed again. Process stems horizontally, paint or spray and assemble the whole.

*Hedge mustard*—Flower insignificant, preserved mostly for foliage.

*Hollyhock*—Face up; two weeks. Cut all full-blown, half-blown and buds showing color, close to the central stem. Use no pins. Remove large leaves, insert pins and process singly. Process remaining stem with small leaves and green buds left on. Paint all greens and reassemble flowers and leaves at appropriate places. Flowers require only a dab of glue.

*Hyacinth*—Face up; two weeks. A simple flower to do. Cut off flower head, apply pins. Stem and spear foliage (if any) need not be processed. Stain stem and foliage and add flower head.

*Indian paintbrush*—Face up; two weeks. Flowers include red, orange and pink shades. I consider the brilliant red shades to be the most outstanding. This is another specimen of coarse and somewhat sticky texture. A thorough brushing of selfsame-colored powdered chalk will not only overcome this tendency of sand to stick to the flower but will also enhance its color. Cut flower head. Use pins. Process stems. Paint all green parts and apply flower heads.

*Leopard lily*—This is the wild Fritillaria. Use no chalk as it will cover up the spots, its most distinguishing feature and from which it gets its name. Cut flower head. Use pins. Face up; two weeks. Reassemble with stem.

*Lewisia*—A ravishing beauty from the Montana lands which somewhat resembles the cactus flower in texture and color, but is more sensitive to humidity than the latter. Do not use chalk. Insert pins. Face up; three weeks. Spray for humidity and reassemble on stem.

*Locoweed* (Utah)—This lovely prostrate plant is found in abundance on the dry low hills in Utah in early spring. The gray-green foliage makes a perfect foil for the rosy-purple flowers. Cut entire plant close to the ground. Cut flower heads. Use pins. Face up; two weeks. No chalking is necessary. Sift correctly colored chalk over entire remaining plant. Process in its entirety. The soft wool-like texture of the leaves requires no spray or further treatment. Apply flowers to dried plant.

*Lupine* (Yellow)—A delightful plant of both foliage and flower. Cut flower clusters and dust thoroughly with yellow chalk. Use pins. Face up; two weeks. Process foliage and stems in usual manner. Spray green and apply flowers whose green parts have been painted.

*Milkweed*—The flower has dramatic form and coloring when fresh. You can expect some change in coloring when dried. Use no chalk as this would destroy its unusual markings. Cut flower heads. Use pins. Face up; two weeks. I have used the dried flower heads in certain arrangements but have never tried to preserve the foliage. It should present no unforeseen problems, however.

*Wild Material*

*Monkey flower*—Gets its name from the unusual markings on the small snapdragon-like flower. The flower is yellow, so for prolonged exhibition it should be chalked, even though this does obliterate some of the delicate markings. Some of these can be restored by spraying with the moisture-proofing spray after the flowers are dried. Use no pins. Face up; two weeks. Process foliage and stems. Spray or paint, then apply flowers.

*Monkshood*—Process in the same way as delphinium.

*Morning glory*—This little prostrate plant is considered a pest by most people and if not controlled will indeed choke out everything in its path. Yet a complete plant, with its graceful trailing habit and delicate pink and white flowers, is a definite addition to any wild flower collection. Cut flowers as close as possible to mother stem. Use no chalk or pins. Face up; three weeks. Process the vines in their entirety, retaining both buds and leaves. Paint or spray green and apply the flowers with glue. The ends of the vines can be cemented together to form a complete plant.

*Mountain ash*—Obviously only a branch is suitable for drying. Cut flower clusters. Use pins. Face up; two weeks. Process remainder of branch in usual manner. Suggest painting leaves rather than spraying so that the dark stems can be retained. Attach flowers. The orange-red berries are most attractive in the fall, but they shrink and shrivel up when dried. I know of no way to prevent this.

*Mullein*—A stately stalk that lends itself beautifully to certain types of flower arranging when dry. The insignificant small flowers appear in patches along the stalk and are not distinguished for their beauty or symmetry. I prefer letting them go to seed and then cutting the stalk in the fall when it has all turned a golden brown. Stand it upright until dry.

## Wild Material

*Ocotillo*—I have had only one opportunity to preserve this desert beauty. I found that it made little difference
whether I submerged it in sand or stood it upright in a container
to air dry. I suggest a brushing with red powdered chalk on the
flowers when fresh to help preserve their fiery color.

*Onions*—Preservation process the same as for hya-
cinths.

*Oregon grape*—The wild variety that grows on the
mountainsides is valuable for its rich coloring in the fall. The
plant is small and low-growing. The flowers that appear in the
spring are insignificant so wait until fall before harvesting. Process
in sand for two weeks as individual leaves. They can be used
singly in arrangements or assembled as a complete plant, as the
need may be.

*Pearly everlasting*—No work here. Gather flowers
in late summer when they are at their peak of bloom. Hang upside down to dry. They are truly everlasting.

*Pentstemon* (blue)—This is one of the loveliest blue
flowers in existence. Process entire stalk, leaves, flowers, and all
in a tall, narrow container, either face up or face down, depending on direction of bells. Paint foliage and stem green when dry.

*Phlox* (common)—All phlox is tricky to do and this
wild form is no exception. After many trials and errors, I have
found that the simplest and most direct approach is the easiest.
The plant is small and compact so cut it close to the ground. Remove all flowers and brush the face of each with powdered chalk,
then process the entire collection in one large shallow container.
Face down; three weeks. Sift properly colored chalk several
times over entire remaining plant. The natural color is gray-
green, unlike any available spray and presents too much of a
problem to paint. Process entire plant in adequate-sized container.

When flowers are dry, place face down on wax paper and
brush backs (not faces) with Flower Sculpture Formula. Allow

to dry thoroughly then glue them back on plant in natural positions. This may seem like an unusual amount of work for this little plant but it will be rewarding in the long run. The tiny flowers are very susceptible to moisture and even spraying will not prevent their drooping. By reinforcing and stiffening their back surfaces, they have no choice but to remain intact while their faces remain soft and velvety looking.

*Poppy* (prickly)—This is one of the most beautiful white flowers I have ever seen. Use no chalk as they retain their crinkly whiteness without it. Use pins if foliage is required. Face up; two weeks. A thorough brushing of the foliage with baby talcum powder will help prevent the sand from clinging to the prickly stems and leaves. Again it is questionable whether the correct color of spray paint can be acquired for the foliage. It would be better to mix oil paints of the right colors with enough turpentine to make a rather thin consistency. Dip a camel's hair brush in the paint, touch it to the foliage and stem letting it spread of its own accord. Add flowers when dry.

*Poppy* (California)—This bit of sunshine has eluded all of my efforts to preserve it. The form and texture is retained but the color fades to a white in short time. Next year I intend to treat the flower with a coating of Flower Sculpture Formula, tinted orange. I suggest that the reader try the same. Face up two weeks before treating with formula. See chapter on Flower Sculpture.

*Pussy willow*—Cut them and use them. They require no care.

*Queen Anne's lace*—Cut flower heads, use pins. Face down; two weeks. Process remaining stems and foliage in the usual manner. Spray and join flower heads to stems.

*Rose* (Spalding's)—Larger than the common wild rose and more difficult to find. Cut flower, use pins. Face up; two weeks. Spray for humidity. Process foliage in usual manner and spray green. Fasten flowers on where they grew.

*Wild Material*

*Rose* (wild)—These lovely flowers are among my favorites. Cut them in all stages of bloom. Do not use pins or dye. The flowers turn somewhat darker when they emerge from the sand, but over a period of time, will fade to the original old rose shade. Face up; two weeks. Spray for humidity. I strongly advise using rose perfume on these to restore their charm. Process foliage, spray green and glue on flowers.

*Sagebrush*—Cut and stand upright to dry. Spray with clear plastic spray to prevent shattering.

*Sand lily*—This is a beautiful subject that requires great care. The fragrant white lilies turn pink as they fade but there is a way to capture them before this happens. Cut the plants very close to the ground very early in the morning, the earlier the better, before the buds open. Get home with them as quickly as possible and immediately cut off the mature buds, retaining all the stem possible. Put these buds in water and stand in strong light, but not direct sunlight. As soon as they open, and they will, process them as directed. Face up; three weeks. When done spray for humidity. In the meantime, cut remaining buds and spent flowers and process them in the same way. Use no pins and no dye. Process entire remaining plant as a unit. When dry, paint to retain natural color. Apply flowers and buds with a dab of glue at base of plant. You will have a beautiful composition when it is finished.

*Sego lily* (Utah state flower)—So named because the Mormon pioneers lived on the bulbs of the plants during their early harrowing days in the Western wilderness. The flower is difficult to do. It comes out of the sand in a semi-transparent condition but a thorough brushing with white powdered chalk before processing will help to correct this. Cut flower, leaving about an inch of stem on the flower. Use pins. Face up; two weeks. The flower has a tendency to shatter when removed from the sand. Never mind; if you want them badly enough, you can easily glue the parts together (three petals only) plus stamens and sepals. The flower will probably require another brushing with chalk after it is dried. This will cloud the deep mahogany markings at the base of the flower. Use a tiny camel's hair brush dipped in a thin oil paint of exactly the correct color to touch up the powdered spots. Add remaining length of stem. There is rarely any foliage found with sego lilies. The happiest and most natural combination is with sagebrush, because that is where they grow.

*Steershead bleeding heart*—A minute plant which is extremely difficult to find. The tiny flower heads are brown and white and resemble the skeleton of a steer's head, hence their name. Cut the flower, stem and all, close to the base. Use no pins or chalk. Face up or horizontal; two weeks. The delicate fern-like foliage can be preserved with care and sprayed green. Apply flower stem with glue at the base of the plant.

*Sunflower*—Process in the same way as the balsams. If a petal or two drops when uncovering, glue them back on. Reinforce all the petals with diluted glue from the center.

*Sweet pea* (Utah)—Cut off flower heads. Face up; two weeks. Use pins if flower stems are thick enough to accept them. Process foliage in usual manner, taking great care to preserve its tendrils and graceful lines. Spray green and apply flower heads with glue.

*Teasel*—An interesting burr-like plant which dries by itself. Flower heads are tan, but may be sprayed any color for arrangements.

*Thistle*—Cut flower heads from plant. Use pins, dust entire green surfaces with baby talcum powder to keep the sand from sticking. Face up; two weeks. Remaining plant may be cut in sections and processed individually. Reassemble and paint or spray green.

*Violet*—Cut the stems as close to the base as possible, leaving the flowers on the stems. Brush flower faces with

## Wild Material

powdered chalk. Several can be processed in one container. Horizontal; two weeks. Spray for humidity. Process leaves in layers, spray or paint leaves and apply flower stems at base with glue.

*Wild strawberry*—No pins or chalk required. Process as for violets.

*Yarrow*—Cut stems as long as desired leaving flower heads on. Hang upside down to dry. Flower heads may be dipped in liquid dye or left plain. Spray with clear plastic spray to prevent shattering. Process foliage in usual manner. Spray green.

*Yucca*—Cut flowers close to central stalk. Use no pins. Face up; one month. After flowers are removed from sand, spray for humidity and hang upside down with clothes pins for further drying. The dried flowers will take on a parchment color. If you wish you may give them a coating of Flower Sculpture Formula to help them retain their white color. Foliage is processed horizontally and takes one month.

*Grasses*—Squirrel-tail, orchard, horsetail, cheat, Indian rice, crested wheat, penny-cress and other grasses are preserved by hanging upside down in clumps to dry. Spray or paint to preserve color. Squirrel-tail and others of a plumy nature should be given a spraying with clear plastic spray to prevent shattering. Grasses are most effective when combined with flowering plant specimens to simulate the growing conditions of their native environment.

### Mounting Specimens for Museum Display

After a specimen is finished and ready for mounting, cut a square piece of heavy cardboard, as large as the breadth of the plant. Mix up a batch of spackle to the consistency of modeling clay. Form it in a mound in the center of the cardboard and let it stand until it begins to get firm, but not hard. Press the stems of your prepared plant material all the way down through the mound until they are resting on the cardboard. Allow the

spackle to become completely dry; twenty-four hours is sufficient. Brace the plant, if necessary, until it stands firmly by itself.
When dry, brush Elmer's Glue on a portion of the surface, starting with the stem area. While the glue is still wet, spoon sifted
dirt over the wet surface, using care not to get any on the flowers
and leaves. Now tip cardboard to one side to allow excess dirt to
slide off and escape. The glued surface will retain a smooth coating of soil. Repeat process on another section until all of the
cardboard has been covered. Allow to dry for about an hour,
then extra rocks, coarse gravel, driftwood or dried bark may be
applied with a dab of glue to add to the plant's natural appearance.

When everything is completely dry, place in a cardboard box
which is slightly larger than the plant. Secure all four corners to
bottom of the box with strips of gum tape. Close or seal the box.
It can now be transported to its destination without danger of
breakage.

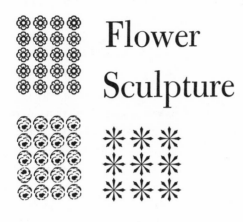

# CHAPTER XV

# Flower
# Sculpture

The candying of fresh flowers is an art whose beginning goes back to ancient days in history and which probably reached its culmination during Elizabethan times. We can only guess why it has become a lost art to the average homemaker of this era. Perhaps the time and effort involved was too much to contemplate in view of the fact that the instant availability of sweets and confections in the modern market was so varied in kinds and quantities. But there seems to have been a rebirth of interest in this lovely art during the past few years. Perhaps it is the continual search for "something new" that has caused this renaissance of taste. And why not? What is more natural than that the three senses of sight, smell and taste should come together to produce that delectable confection of old, the candied flower?

The recipes for the candying or crystallizing of flowers are many and varied. The old ones almost always resorted to a syrup method with slight differences and variations. The more modern ones, with an eye to time and effort, advocate a coating of egg white and granulated sugar. Both produce a candied petal of sorts but each has its shortcomings. The syrup method tends to shrink and distort the petal and results in a radical change in color, so that in the end you have a sugared "something," perhaps tasting somewhat like the marriage of the flowers and sugar but suffering in appearance because the natural contour is gone. It can however be kept indefinitely.

On the other hand, the egg white and granulated sugar method preserves the exact contour of the petal but by reason of the egg white, must be refrigerated and then can be kept only for a limited time.

With these shortcomings in mind, I am presenting a method for candying flowers that surmounts these difficulties and is superior to all others that I have tried to the extent that in the finished product you have a flower that looks as it did in nature, of true color and contour, that is deliciously edible and will last indefinitely without refrigeration. Furthermore, the aesthetic possibilities for its use are greatly expanded. Under this method, not only lifelike flowers can be obtained, but whole bouquets of edible flowers. They will not only whet the appetite but when combined with greens can grace the table as a centerpiece and can be used for other decorative purposes.

After trying out and rejecting many formulas for candying flowers, I came across an old English recipe using acacia gum in the candying process that made sense. I offer it here in all of its old English charm:

> To candy Flowers or Greens in Branches with Gum Arabic, steep your Gum Arabic in Water, wet the Flowers in it and shake them in a Cloth that they may be dry; then dip them in fine sifted Sugar and hang them on a String tied across a Chimney that hath a Fire in it; They must hang two or three Days till the Flowers be quite dry.
> *From The Recipe Book Of Mrs. Mary Eales*
> *Confectioner to Queen Anne—1718*

I have no chimney that hath a fire in it, but out of this quaint bit of information, I have developed a recipe that works. Here it is:

Acacia gum or gum arabic, though rather difficult to find, is safely edible and is sometimes used in the making of candies and liquid medicines, such as cough syrups, etc. If your druggist doesn't stock it, he can either get it for you or indicate where it

*Flower Sculpture*

is available. Get the powdered variety which comes in a one-pound can and costs about $2.60. I suggest that you mix up a small batch for practice until you get the feel of the thing.

Measure 3 level teaspoons of acacia gum and add 3 teaspoons of cold water. Mix in a small bowl or teacup and when partly dissolved, set the bowl in a shallow pan of water on the stove. Allow the water in the pan to come to a boil. Let it stand and boil 2 or 3 minutes then turn the heat off and let it stand in the hot water for another 5 minutes. Stir contents of cup thoroughly. Now remove cup from pan of water and allow mixture to cool. Skim off all of the foamy top and it is ready to use.

Have ready about ½ cup of granulated sugar on a platter or dinner plate, a *new*, clean camel's hair brush of medium thickness, several pieces of paper kitchen toweling and the flowers you wish to candy. They should be small flowers such as rosebuds, small full-blown roses, violets, sprigs of lilac, individual florets of stock, forget-me-nots, geranium florets, nasturtiums, etc. Larger flowers may be attempted after you have had experience with the smaller ones.

Dip the entire flower in the mixture, making sure all parts are submerged. Swish it around a little. Lift the flower out by its short stem and let the excess syrup drip off for a few seconds. Now place the flower face down on the paper toweling and brush the petals outward with the camel's hair brush, squeezing out the mixture from between and on the petals. This also serves to distribute the coating on hidden and close-packed parts. Blot again on paper towels. Turn the flower face up and sprinkle granulated sugar over all surfaces. I said sprinkle, not pour. Separate petals with a toothpick and sprinkle sugar between them. Do this all around. Last, sprinkle back surfaces and hang by the stem with a clothespin face down to dry. It should take about 4 or 5 hours for this to be accomplished. The happy result should be a lifelike-looking flower, true in color and form with a frosted look. (See colored pictures of individual flowers preserved by this method.)

Edible leaves may be treated the same way. Violet, mint and nasturtium leaves are especially attractive and when arranged on a plate with assorted candied flowers make an unusual and color-

‡‡ 145 ‡‡

Candied flowers, from right to left: wild rose, geranium, nasturtium, white lilac, violet, blue delphinium (not edible), fairy rose, fuchsia, stock, yellow rose bud.

ful after-dinner tidbit to serve at a special party. Of course, it goes without saying that all this should be done under the most exacting of sanitary conditions, if they are to be eaten.

If they are made for decorations only, their uses are many. Combine them with tulle, ribbons or greenery to decorate gift packages, tiny nosegays for party favors, or to decorate birthday gift packages and birthday or party desserts. My favorite dessert is a violet sherbet topped with a candied violet, while on one side of the dessert plate rests a violet leaf holding several violets, all candied and frosty looking. Whole candied pink peony petals could encase a mound of pink ice cream and can be nibbled instead of the usual accompanying cookies or cake. They can be combined with tiny miniature candy fruits, edible also, and arranged in a compote or they could be made in garlands for holiday decorating or used to form a miniature Della Robbia Christmas tree. The recipe and directions for making these miniature fruits, follows below and is quite easy to do.

### THE CANDY FORMULA

Procure a package of large gumdrops. (The white ones are best because they are free from coloring and flavoring and you are going to add your own as the need arises, but the other colors need not be discarded because uses for them will be found according to the effects you wish to achieve.) Pick out 10 pieces of the candy and put them in hot water and wash off all the coating of granulated sugar with which they are covered. You may have to use several waters to accomplish this. They must be smooth and free from grit. Cut them up into small pieces with either a knife or kitchen shears. Put them in a small sauce pan with about 5 tablespoons of water. Bring them to a brisk boil and continue boiling until the water begins to be absorbed, stirring all the while. Continue to add water, a little at a time, from time to time as needed. Lower the heat; do not let them burn or dry out. They are done when they are completely dissolved and the whole has turned into a thick jelly-like mass. Empty contents into a large bowl and gradually pour in powdered sugar. The amount is indeterminate, but it should be in the neighborhood of 2½ cups, depending upon the gumdrop liquid. Knead this with your hands until a thick dough is obtained of about the consistency of molding clay. It must not be soft enough to stick to your hands yet not stiff enough to crumble. Wrap in a damp cloth and put on a dish. This then, is your basic recipe and can be broken up in small quantities, flavored and colored as the requirements arise.

There are many uses for this "dough" candy. It can be used for molding fruits, figurines and even flowers without the aid of any substructure and dries to a smooth hard state. All that is required is the will and the imagination. To make the fruit, pinch off a piece of the candy about the size of the piece of fruit that you want to simulate. (Miniatures are easier and generally more desirable.) If your candy is dry to the point of crumbling, dampen it with wet fingers, then knead it a bit for even and smooth consistency. If it is too sticky, add more powdered sugar and knead that well into the mixture. Flavor to taste. Then with the hands dusted with powdered sugar, roll it as hard as you can between the palms of both hands until it becomes a smooth round ball without cracks or lumps. (This is the procedure to follow in every case, regardless of the shape of the fruit you are trying to produce). Now gently mold it into the shape of the fruit. In the case of the banana, it should be gently elongated, narrowed at one end and slightly curved. Insert a toothpick or wire in the large end to a depth of about ¼ inch and stick the pick upright in a piece of styrofoam until the candy has dried.

If an apple is to be made, again pinch off a piece, roll it into a round ball, stick a whole clove in at any point, making sure to

*Flower Sculpture*

insert the toothpick at the end directly opposite the clove. In the case of the apple, the insertion of the toothpick or wire in the soft candy will be sufficient to make the naturalistic stem indentation in the fruit.

The pear should be slightly more elongated than the apple, keeping the bottom half round as the apple, then gradually tapering off to the smaller half of the fruit. Insert a clove in the bottom of the large round half and the toothpick in the smaller stem end.

Oranges, of course, would be left round. However, the proper skin surface effect may be produced by making tiny indentations all over its surface with the prongs of a small fork or nutpick. Insert the toothpick at any point and set it up to dry. Plums, peaches, and apricots are simply the original round balls with creases down one side made with a toothpick as deeply as desired. Lemons are smaller balls that have been elongated with tiny semi-knobs formed at each end. Grapes and cherries are smaller balls still, and in each a very fine wire is inserted and when finished are twisted together to form clusters. In the latter case, however, the wires will not be sufficiently strong to hold the fruit upright while it is drying so the wire should be bent over a taut line with the fruit hanging down until dry.

The strawberry is more complicated but is so realistic that it warrants a trial run, after which you will want to make loads of them. But the procedure varies somewhat from the other fruits. First make some green hulls or calyxes. These can be made from green crepe paper or cotton cloth. Cut a small circle from the green material about ¾ inch in diameter, fold it in fourths, cut 2 V-shaped notches in the lower edge, through all 4 thicknesses, equidistant from both sides of the folded material. Unfold and punch a hole in the center. Set aside until needed. Now mold the candy into the shape of a strawberry and insert a toothpick in the larger calyx end. Make small indentations all over the berry with the small end of a toothpick to receive and hold the seeds which are to be added later. Paint the berry with undiluted red food coloring on the very end opposite the calyx end; now a little yellow beyond this and toward the red. Then with a semiwet brush, blend all the three colors into each other, the yellow into the green, the red into the yellow, etc. While the candy is still wet put celery seeds in the depressions already made with the toothpick. This can be done by dipping the end of a toothpick in water and then onto the seed. If the toothpick is wet the seed will adhere to it and can then be transferred to the small depression ready to receive it. The seed will stick to the surface because the berry is still damp from the food coloring. Last of all, slip the waiting green calyx through the toothpick and press gently onto the end of the berry. It will stick for the same reason.

Raspberries are round balls with a deep cavity made at one point with the round end of a metal nutpick. It is painted pure red or dark blue-purple as the choice may be, rolled in sesame seeds, allowed to dry and then repainted the same color, and allowed to dry again.

Blackberries are small oval balls, painted dark purple, rolled in sesame seeds, painted again and dried in the same manner. An endless variety of fruits can be made by use of the imagination and altering the technique to fit the needs of each type. Specimens of real fruit or in the absence of that, colored pictures from a nursery catalogue will be a great assistance in determining the shape and coloring of each type.

When the candied fruits without the seed covering are dry, they are ready to be painted: apples, red, yellow or green; bananas, yellow diluted with water and allowed to dry, with the black lines and markings made of melted chocolate, applied with a toothpick; pears, green or green-shaded yellow; lemons, yellow; and oranges, orange mixed with yellow (a second coat may be required but only after the first one has completely dried). The purple for plums and grapes can be made by mixing red and blue coloring. In fact, many varying tints and shades that add so much of reality to the appearance of the fruit may be obtained by mixing and diluting colors and color combinations. Here again, a piece of real fruit or colored pictures will be of the greatest assistance.

If the fruits are to be eaten, paint them with pure food coloring only. But if they are to be used for decorative purposes, acrylic poster or any other paints except oils may be used. (Oils refuse to dry.) They can be sprayed with a clear waterproof spray if desired, after they are dry.

The toothpicks can be painted green or simply be left in their natural state and used for anchorage when assembling the fruits with greens or in building a compote; they will prove especially valuable in making wreaths or garlands. In the event the fruits and flowers are destined to be eaten, pull the toothpick out as soon as the coloring has dried and before it adheres tightly to the candy. I like to combine these fruits and flowers with preserved greens, either glycerinized or sand dried and sprayed green for permanency. They can, however, be combined with fresh material if desired. These fruits and flowers, if properly made, will offer a dish of the most delectable sweetmeats you have ever eaten. But just go ahead and eat one! I dare you to do it! But others will and I can see you now, shuddering, as your friends consume with delight these little masterpieces of sculptured art that you have so faithfully and lovingly made.

### FLOWER SCULPTURE FORMULA

Now comes the most important and useful contribution to the art of flower preservation to come out of this experimentation with acacia gum and powdered sugar. I call it the Flower Sculpture Formula. Note the name well because you will find it referred to many times in this book and if you wish to preserve some of the heretofore "untouchables," you will need to know how to mix it and use it. Without it some of the wild flowers such as the balsam, phlox and globe mallow could not have been brought under control. It works wonders on some of the cultivated varieties also—flowers that need special treatment in order to keep their contour and color. I have reason to believe that the elusive lily of the valley, hyacinth, daffodil and other flowers that have been only partially successful by my standards will respond very well to this treatment. I intend to try them all next year.

Here is the formula. Follow the mixing exactly as directed: Into a small pottery bowl (a teacup is too thin) measure ½ teaspoon of acacia gum and 3 teaspoons of cold water. Mix and let stand ½ hour. Set the bowl in a shallow pan of cold water and let the water in the pan come to a boil, stirring the contents of the bowl all the while. Remove the pan from the stove but let the bowl remain in the hot water for a few minutes longer while you measure out 9 level teaspoons of powdered sugar. Remove the bowl from the hot water and add the measured powdered sugar. Stir until dissolved. Allow to stand until the syrup is cool. Skim all the surface carefully and completely. Add 3 level teaspoons of Liquitex Matte Varnish (which is available at most art supply stores; it is put out in bottles of 8 fluid ounces and costs $1.25). Mix thoroughly with syrup and add a few drops of food coloring for desired tint. THIS IS NOT TO BE PUT ON EDIBLE FLOWERS. It is a coating to preserve the form, color, and markings of display flowers that do not completely respond to ordinary treatment and it does give the flower a realistic but sculptured look. IT IS NOT TO BE USED ON FRESH FLOWERS. The flowers must have been sand dried before it can be applied and it is best to give the flowers a light spraying with moisture-proofing spray, and allow them to dry before coating them with the formula.

The size of the flower is of no importance but if the petals overlap or even touch one another, it is advisable to gently pull off the petals, using care not to tear them. Paint *one* side only of each petal with the formula, making sure that you do cover the entire surface and that you don't leave any bare spots. Keep the brush well saturated with the formula but at the same time don't use too much on the flower. The best way that I can describe it is to use enough to coat the petal thoroughly but not enough to run in streaks or bead up in drops. Lay the petal dry side down on wax paper, and proceed to the next ones until they are all finished. Let them get perfectly dry (about 2 hours) then turn them over and coat the other sides. When both sides are thoroughly dry, they may be glued back on the flower head with a bit of Duco glue.

The flowers will have a shiny surface for several weeks but this will gradually disappear and after about a month they will resume their natural appearance. The petals will be stiff and able to withstand humidity and they will keep the color, markings and veinings that were visible on the uncoated flower. The coating will not show. The colors may even be changed or darkened by this process if you so desire; the color change will be determined by the amount of coloring that you put in the formula. Do not try to put light colors over a natural dark flower, but you may put a darker tint over a light one. Coat the flower only one time. If you give it a second treatment, the color streaks and the coating becomes visible. Pour the unused portion in a small bottle and keep it tightly corked. It will last for several months. But if upon reopening the bottle, you discover that a thick rubbery coating has formed on the top, discard it and mix up a new batch. Since it is somewhat difficult to find gum arabic or acacia and because it is a bit tricky to mix (absolutely level measurements, correct temperature and proper skimming), Elizabeth Cole has consented to make it in her laboratories, so if you wish you can order it already mixed. Six one-ounce bottles, one each of white, yellow, red, pink, blue and lavender, can be ordered postpaid in the United States at $6.00 a box. Colors may be made darker by adding a drop or two of food coloring. The formula will last for several months if the bottles are kept tightly closed. Address: Elizabeth Cole, Inc., 3336 South 23rd East, Salt Lake City, Utah 84109.

Unfortunately I cannot give a complete list of the flowers that respond to this treatment because I developed it only three or four months ago and have not yet had the opportunity to test it on as many flowers as I should have desired. But the serious flower dryer will have the fun of experimenting for herself and can make up her own list as the flowers appear in their respective seasons.

# CHAPTER XVI

# The Arrangement

Flower arranging is an art in itself and deserves to be treated as such. But then so is flower preservation. They are the two halves that comprise the whole. To devote one's time and energy to preserving the materials and then not to know what to do with them is very much like buying an expensive material for a gown and then leaving it around unmade, or using it for a house dress. So if you don't know how to arrange your flowers, only half of the distance has been covered.

But since this book is primarily concerned with preparing the material that goes into the arrangement, we cannot go into the details of arranging. Many books have been written on the subject and there are numerous teachers and classes available in almost every town and city in the country. My advice to the pupil is to take advantage of them. By all means enroll in a class, visit flower shows, read books on the subject and start a scrapbook of pictures of arrangements for your own use. Not that I advise copying someone else's work—your arrangement must be your own and it must express your creative talent. But you will learn, along with other things, how certain arrangers handle various materials, combinations of colors, harmony, balance, proportion, contrast, gradation, unity, form and line. In short, all of the principles of good design will be illustrated, if done by an expert, so study them well, and like a good bridge player, learn the rules of the game first, and then learn when to break them and for what purpose. But pay heed to the advice of the Japanese, who are masters of this art, and be relaxed in your approach to flower arranging. Don't sit down with a yardstick or measuring tape in order to *make* your material conform to the rules. If you do the result will be stiff and lifeless and will resemble a painting done by filling in numbered spaces. Let the plant material itself guide you and be your inspiration. Then and then only will you enjoy it and truly express yourself.

Generally speaking, the same principles with one or two exceptions apply both to fresh and to preserved flowers. More material, for example, and for several reasons, is required for a preserved arrangement. Flowers will have shrunk a little. Some stems will have been stripped of their foliage so that extra material will be necessary to cover up the bare spots.

Then, too, more substantial anchoring is necessary for preserved flowers. It must be remembered that every speck of moisture has been drawn from the bloom and stems, so that they end up as light as feathers. Unless anchored firmly, they are likely to topple over and get broken.

I use sand to anchor flowers in a tall opaque vase and a mound of floral clay to anchor them in a shallow one. If the arrangement is to be especially large and heavy and if the bowl will permit, I very often use both materials for greater safety.

There are some advantages that preserved material has over the fresh counterpart, such as its long lasting quality. It has always seemed a sad thing to me that despite all the time, study and work that go into an arrangement of fresh flowers, they wither and die in such a short time. But if your material has been preserved, you can not only take unlimited time in arranging them without the danger of wilting, but the finished composition will last for years, thus giving you prolonged enjoyment of it plus a more rewarding compensation for your efforts.

Then too, there is more latitude in their use. Preserved flowers, unless their colors are altered, have a tendency to take on a muted tone. I have placed arrangements of varicolored hollyhocks in homes of every color scheme imaginable, except yellow and orange. In each case, the flowers melted into the background as if they had been done especially for the particular room.

Left, sand used to anchor preserved flower; right, shallow bowl holds mound of floral clay for anchoring.

On the other hand, one disadvantage, if you call it such, is the fact that you must sometimes know in advance what use you wish to make of the material before it is preserved. A good teacher will show you how to manipulate and bend fresh stems and branches in order to achieve a certain line, such as the Hogarth Curve. This is not difficult to do when you are working with fresh material because it is soft and pliable. Not so with dried material: once it is dried it must remain in the position it assumed when it went into the sand. But if you can foresee its use and know the angle you wish it to take, it can be bent, wired and preserved in that position. The branch won't like this and will try to rebel but do it anyhow. Show it who is the boss.

Also more care must be used in the actual arranging of preserved material than with fresh forms. The latter will tolerate manipulating. It won't make much difference to a fresh flower if, when placing it in the arrangement, you accidently brush it against another flower or leaf, nor will it object if you happen to bend a petal backward; once freed, it immediately flops back in place with no apparent damage done. Not so with preserved material—even an accidental brushing against a leaf may break it and flower petals will also break off if forced in the wrong direction. I am of the opinion that professional flower arrangers should learn how to preserve flowers before accepting an assignment to arrange material that someone else has lovingly and carefully prepared. Thus undue damage and loss can be cut to a minimum. The bond is inseparable and each can learn from the other.

An important point to remember also is that the container can be just about as important as the arrangement and indeed is a part of the arrangement, so make sure that it is not only appropriate for the material that you wish to put in it, but also for the room—and place in the room—that it is to occupy. A gorgeous bouquet in a tawdry container can be in as bad taste as a beautiful evening gown on a woman wearing sneakers. And make sure you select a container that you can spare. It should not be one that you are dependent upon for other uses. Remember that these arrangements are more or less permanent acquisitions and they will not tolerate being moved in and out of containers at will.

Before I consider an arrangement of preserved flowers finished I like to restore its one lost charm—its perfume. For many years this lost attribute has worried me because the more perfect and appealing your bouquet looks, the more people are inclined to bend down to sniff its fragrance; to all appearances this should be there, yet it is not, and invariably a look of disappointment comes over their faces. Now this fragrance can be restored, but not with just any perfume; that won't do. Elizabeth Cole, perfumer, of Elizabeth Cole, Inc., 3336 South 23rd East, Salt Lake City, Utah, has long studied this need and has succeeded in recapturing the haunting fragrance of the rose and a combination of fragrances for the mixed bouquet. She has produced these from imported oils. They come in three fragrances, one dram of each in a box and the box sells for $3.50. One or two drops on the heart of the flower will restore its subtle perfume and will last for months. So no more do these lovely creatures have to hang their heads in embarrassment because of the loss of this haunting charm. Now, as my friends bend over to smell the flower, they exclaim, "Why, you have even preserved its perfume!"

Sometimes I like to give an arrangement still another extra touch. A butterfly may make the ensemble look really natural and very gardenish. And butterflies are not hard to come by or to prepare. Armed with a butterfly net, any preserver can go traipsing about the garden catching her own. Or you can hire little boys in the neighborhood to net them. I pay five cents for little butterflies and ten cents for the big ones. Also, there are commercial firms that sell butterflies from all lands.

Once one of the creatures is in hand, the rest is simple. Hold it by the wings, being careful not to hurt or crush it and put a dab of cotton saturated with any kind of cleaning fluid to its "nose." It "goes to sleep" instantly. The only difficulty sometimes is that the wings will fold up. If your desire is to have them open in a V, simply slip one wing between the pages of a book and gently close the book. This leaves the body and other wing free to dangle but pointing mostly upward. After several days reverse the wings, giving each of them a day or two in the book. Several days (two to four) in this press will make the position of the wings permanent, and you then will have a butterfly with the appearance of being eternally in flight. The last step is to put the dab of glue on the butterfly's abdomen and stick it to a petal. The butterfly will last as long as the flowers, perhaps even longer. And the effect, of course, is enchanting.

There is one final duty to be performed once an arrangement is completed and placed on the piano, mantel or coffee or dining table. That is to guard it zealously against the itching fingers of your friends. Most people will want to give it "just a little pinch." Don't let them! The admonition must be: "Admire but don't touch." If you permit your arrangement to be fingered, you must be prepared to say good-bye to your flowers.

### Flowers Under Glass Bells

Another way to display your arrangements is to put them under glass bells. The reasons why this might be advantageous are that the bells provide an added protection against humidity and dust. Also the risk of breakage is lessened when small children and pets are around. Or you might wish to achieve the Victorian look. If so encase your flowers under glass by all means. The Victorians did this but their flowers were usually made of silk, wax, beads, etc. How much better preserved flowers would look than artificial ones!

Of course this is practical only with comparatively small arrangements. The cost and availability of glass bells of large size would be prohibitive except for museums and state houses, when the arrangement is of such size and value as to warrant a specially constructed dome.

In any case, when a glass bell is used, large or small, it should be hermetically sealed. Either tape or glue the bell to its wooden base in order to keep it from being tipped over and to insure the maximum protection for your flowers.

## *Transportation of Arrangements*

There are certain ironclad rules to follow in the event you wish to move an arrangement from one house to another or ship it out of town:

> 1. Never try to gift wrap a bouquet; you will break your flowers. They must be carried to their destination in their container, unwrapped, by a responsible person if it is in the same city. It takes 2 people to accomplish this: one to carry the flowers, the other to drive the car. No one can drive a car and successfully take care of an arrangement of flowers at the same time.
> 2. Use care when getting in and out of cars that you don't brush the flowers against the doors, break the tall ones against the car roof or hold them too close to you when entering or leaving the car. Let the driver open and close the doors.
> 3. Instruct the driver to turn corners slowly and not to apply brakes too suddenly.
> 4. Never transport flowers during windy or rainy weather. Dry cold won't hurt them but wind and rain will.

Out-of-town shipping is a risky business but it can be done with a fair chance of the arrangements getting to their destination without too much damage, if the following instructions are carried out:

*The Arrangement*

1. Never attempt to ship flowers during the rush of the holiday season.

2. Small arrangements only should be sent and then only after the following careful preparations: The container should be in the form of a compote, something with a foot on it as this makes for easier anchoring. Before the arrangement is packaged, it will be necessary to pour melted paraffin wax over the clay in the container in order to prevent any of the stems from slipping out, in case the package is turned upside down. The wax may be tinted green, if so desired, by adding a piece of green wax crayon while it is being melted. Or, you may simply melt up a green candle.

3. Select a heavy cardboard box which is somewhat larger and taller than the arrangement. Cut down through two corners of one side, from the top of the box to the bottom, but leaving the bottom intact and fastened to the box. Procure two flexible but strong pieces of wire of considerable length. Hold them together and twist them tightly together several times at about the middle of their length. Place this twisted part on one side of the stem of the container at its narrowest point. Now separate the wires of the untwisted half and stretch one on and around each side of the stem and again twist them together, thus tightly encasing the stem. Slide the container in the box, in its center, and draw an outline around the foot of the container. Remove the arrangement and pierce two holes through the bottom of the box, on the outline, but directly opposite each other. Replace the arrangement. The long dangling ends of the wires must be inserted in the holes, two in one hole and two in the other, drawn through, tightened and securely fastened to the outside bottom of the box. This should hold the arrangement securely and prevent it from slipping around or moving. Tape up the open·side of the box and the lid. Make sure it is strong and substantial. Wrap with heavy paper and string. Make sure that the recipient knows how to remove the arrangement when it arrives. This consists of cutting down through all four corners, from top to bottom, cutting the wire and care-

fully removing the arrangement. Do not attempt to ship loose material.

## Don't Throw Your Old Flowers Away

No, don't throw them away. They may be dusty, faded and drab looking, but if they have that one characteristic left—contour—they can be renovated and saved.

Recently I decided to clear out my stock of old unused flowers, the neglected ones that had been stored in the back of my shelves for at least ten years. I was tired of looking at them and I needed the space for some newcomers. Needless to say they were a sorry-looking sight—dusty, faded and covered with cobwebs. Then a thought occurred to me: why not try an experiment to revive them? It worked. This is how I did it.

First I sorted them out, retaining only those whose contours remained intact. I shut my eyes and threw the others away. I decided that a new and fresh approach was necessary to this salvaging operation, so I carried them out of my customary workroom to another part of the house, a room with good light and comfortable working conditions and unhampered by the accumulations of the workroom.

I placed a large pan half filled with clean sand on my lap. Then I removed one flower from its temporary stem and holding it over the pan, I gave it a gentle but thorough sandblasting, letting the sand fall in a stream from the right hand all over the surfaces of the flower, gently shaking and rotating the flower with the left hand as the sand fell on it. Both the back and the front of the flower got the same treatment. I repeated this several times. Then with the flower head pointed downward, I tapped the stem until all of the sand was removed. When I turned it over, I had a perfectly clean flower. The sandblasting had removed all traces of dust, cobwebs and old grains of sand that had been clinging to the flower since it was first preserved. If any of the petals seemed loose, I reinforced them with diluted glue, or if any of them fell off during the cleaning process, I put them back on with undiluted glue.

Next, I gave the flower a light spraying with moisture-proofing spray, the purpose being to prepare the surfaces for the chalk. The dye adheres more readily to a sprayed surface than to a neutral one. The flower was then put back on its temporary stem to dry and I proceeded to clean the rest of the flowers in the same manner.

The technique of the restoration of the color depended upon the type of the flower being treated. If it was a flower with a distinct and outlined center, I brushed each petal with colored chalk of the desired tint, being careful to cover all surfaces evenly with gentle but patient strokes. I advise supporting the petal from underneath while doing this. When I had finished, I went over the petals with a clean brush to remove the excess chalk, then gave it another sandblasting to remove any remaining chalk. I then applied the permanent stem and painted the calyx and stem green. All that remained to be done now was to apply another light coat of spray to remove the chalky look and set the color. When it dried, a few minutes later, I had a flower that looked as if it had been plucked from the garden just minutes ago! And it was already ten years old!

But the real thrill came when I did the multipetaled flowers, such as the double hollyhock. The beauty of this flower is unbelievable when rejuvenated. But here the procedure differs from the brush method. The flower is cleaned in the same manner but never, never must a brush be applied to it. Hold the flower over a large bowl or platter, fill a tea strainer half full of the colored chalk and shake it over the flower in every direction several times. Tap gently to remove chalk. If a deeper shading is desired in the heart of the flower, dip a very fine brush in a darker colored chalk and apply at the appropriate points. Now give the entire flower a gentle sandblasting, tap the stem to remove excess grains and chalk, and spray to set and blend the colors.

I wonder if you would believe me if I were to tell you that double hollyhocks, spiraea, water lilies and many more kinds emerged from this treatment more beautiful than they were ten years ago, when I first preserved them? My proof is that I had a sale of my flowers and the first ones to go were these "old" ones that had been newly rejuvenated. Furthermore, this same procedure can be repeated on these same flowers years from now. Even their colors can be changed to suit your fancy as long as you put a darker shade on a lighter flower—never the reverse.

A practice, somewhat like this, is sometimes carried out in India, when a lovely sari is purchased. It may be embroidered in gold and silver. The women buy a light-colored sari, wear it for a while, then dye it slightly darker. This shade is in turn worn for a while and then again dyed a darker color. This goes on until the material is literally worn out. Then they melt it up and retrieve the gold and silver—quite an investment!

A similar dividend can be had from your garden treasures. Keep the contour intact, clean them well, preserve or change their color and they will be beautiful forever.

# CHAPTER XVII

# Teachers' Manual

The question springs up: where can one go to learn this craft of flower preservation? It is one thing to read about it and quite another to see it done, and like any other subject properly taught, it requires both a teacher and a textbook.

There are no qualified teachers that I know of. I am constantly being beset by requests for classes, which I have given from time to time in the last seven or eight years. But even a preliminary course of six lessons does not qualify one to become a teacher.

Those who would like to teach should know that while the qualifications are not numerous, they are exacting. It goes without saying that they should know the contents of this book in its entirety and have thoroughly mastered and perfected all of the techniques described. But that is only the framework of the structure; in addition, they should acquire the personal experience of preserving as many specimens of horticulture as possible, at least all the common varieties that grow in the average garden. How else can they instruct the pupils in this craft and be able to answer their questions? And the problems will vary according to the locality and climate in which they teach. It becomes evident that teachers cannot be made overnight, but must evolve over a period of time and by hard work and a desire to experiment, before they can pass this accumulated knowledge on to others. In addition, they should acquire some knowledge of flower arranging.

For those who meet these requirements and have a desire to become a teacher, I have outlined a brief sketch of the ground to be covered, with regard to the number of classes, maximum number of pupils, division of subject matter and materials to have on hand. All this is as I teach it. It is not imperative that it be followed to the letter. It is but a suggestion and is flexible enough to be changed if the need arises.

The course consists of six lessons, two hours each, once a week. I have found that a minimum of eight (for profit's sake) and a maximum of 10 pupils is about right. The maximum limitation is set so that each pupil can receive individual instruction. Logically the classes should be set up for and given during the blooming season, to insure as many varied materials as possible with which to work.

LESSON I—Preliminary Work for the Teacher

    A. Provide an adequate workroom. It must be large enough to accommodate pupils and supplies without crowding. The basement is ideal.

    B. Acquire the following supplies:
1. Large work table
2. Sand stock, both washed and unwashed
3. A varied supply of containers
4. Stem supply
5. Specimens of preserved flowers
6. "Mother box" for each pupil
7. Brushes, scissors, pliers, pins, toothpicks, pointed wooden sticks, glue, diluted glue, paint, spray, floral tape, wires, bottle caps, powdered chalk, pencils and pads, liquid dye, precut cardboard pieces for boxes, precut pieces of gummed paper (one set for each pupil), supply of glycerin and water, cans of unwashed sand (one for each pupil), register and receipt book and fresh flowers to process.

    C. Give short preliminary talk describing purpose of work.

D. Explain washing, drying and sifting of sand, allow pupils to participate briefly.
   1. If prepared sand is used, explain process nevertheless

E. Explain need and use of "mother box."

F. Demonstrate proper technique of handling sand.
   1. Have pupils practice using this technique.

G. Explain types of containers and collars.

H. Have each pupil make a container.
   1. Do one side to illustrate how it's done

I. Explain face-up method.

J. Have each pupil cover a single flower face-up—assist and supervise work.

K. Summarize day's work and announce next lesson.

LESSON II—Face Down Method; "Faith" Method; Dyeing Flowers.

A. Assemble materials and necessary flowers.

B. Explain and demonstrate face-down method.

C. Have each pupil cover a flower face down.

D. Explain and demonstrate mound method and give its uses.

E. Have each pupil cover a flower using mound method.

F. Explain and demonstrate "faith" method.

G. Have pupils cover a flower using this method.
   1. If appropriate flowers are not available, demonstrate with previously preserved specimens —care prevents damage.
   2. Use collars if necessary; explain their use

H. Demonstrate use of powdered chalk for dyeing flowers before covering.

     1. Show how to remove excess chalk

     2. Teach artistry of shading

  I. Have pupils dye a flower and cover.

     1. Individual chalk bags not necessary—one will do for all

  J. Have pupils process more flowers.

  K. Clean up and summarize. Suggest pupils bring extra flowers.

  L. If time remains, teach grating and mixing of chalk.

LESSON III—Horizontal; Uncovering; Liquid Dye

  A. Assemble materials and flowers.

     1. Long containers in assorted sizes

  B. Discuss method, reasons, adaptability.

  C. Supervise making sand mounds and inserting cardboard tabs.

  D. Assist each pupil in placing and anchoring flower.

     1. More sand may be needed for anchoring tabs

  E. Inspect and supervise covering flower.

     1. Lower florets first

     2. Maintain natural position

     3. Keep sandbed even

  F. Demonstrate using large container on sheet.

     1. Keep sand supply close by

     2. Give reasons for this procedure

  G. Demonstrate cutting tall spikes in portions, inserting toothpicks, covering one section at a time.

     1. Leave flower stalk in water; start with top section

     2. Explain and demonstrate assembling after material is dried; have on hand a previously dried specimen for this purpose

  H. Demonstrate uncovering process. Let pupils uncover their first flower processed two weeks ago, face-up.

    1. Show how to clean flower, apply diluted glue if necessary, put on temporary stems, stand upright in cans of unwashed sand; reasons

I. Demonstrate flowers best done this way, with the use of liquid dye.

    1. What flowers best done this way

    2. Stress thorough drying of flower before covering.

J. Clean-up, summary, question and criticism period. Warn against careless habits.

LESSON IV—Foliage

A. Materials should include as many types of foliage as possible.

B. Explain and demonstrate exceptions to rule: one to a container.

C. Let pupil cover as many types as possible.

    1. Supervise covering. At this point pupils will have developed their own habits of covering. Watch for errors, particularly holding the hand too high which results in loss of control. Advise them to work closer to the subject being covered.

D. Explain glycerin and water solution.

    1. ½ water and ½ glycerin

E. Have ready large container of solution, submerge appropriate foliage, show finished specimens you have treated this way.

    1. Have pupils keep weekly watch on progress of material being treated

F. Spray preserved foliage to restore color.

G. Explain stem absorption method.

      1. Study some being treated

  H. Give lists of common foliage suitable for each treatment.

   I. Let pupils uncover face-down flowers.
      1. Clean, if time permits
      2. Apply temporary stems

   J. Clean up, summarize, encourage pupils to start drying extra specimens at home.

## LESSON V—Grooming

  A. Assemble materials, including extra stems of varying sizes.

  B. Have pupils uncover all flowers that have completed their drying time.

  C. Have pupils clean, glue and reinforce all flowers that require it.
      1. Stress rule: Straight glue to glue on petals, diluted glue to reinforce petals

  D. Give flowers more dye (powdered chalk only) if needed.
      1. Apply with brush (only)

  E. Explain and demonstrate application of permanent stems.
      1. Flower in stem
      2. Stem in flower
      3. Combination of wire and stem
      4. Flower on original stem (with pin)
      5. Application of flower cluster on branch with pins

  F. Demonstrate wrapping wire stem with floral tape.
      1. Stress rule: *Never wrap real stem; always wrap wire one*

  G. Show how to paint calyx and entire stem, whether real or wire, using properly mixed and diluted green paint.

1. Consistency of thin cream soup

H. Insert in styrofoam or can of unwashed sand until dry.

I. Spray completed flower for stabilization of color (if chalked) and protection from moisture.
1. Moisture-proofing spray

J. Clean up, summarize, and remind pupils to bring flower container and floral clay, also flowers they have done at home.

LESSON VI—Making the Arrangement

A. Previous study of principles of flower arranging necessary for teacher.

B. Show as many colored illustrations of varying styles of flower arrangements as possible.

C. Uncover all remaining material, clean, groom and add stems and spray if necessary.

D. Study containers brought to class, make suggestions as to their requirements.

E. Help pupils form adequate mound of floral clay in containers, pressing edges firmly against bottom of container. Dry Oasis may be used instead of clay, if preferred.

F. Help them establish outline, height, width, lowest level.

G. Stress point of interest.

H. Bend wire stems for graceful lines.

I. Arrange flowers first, then add foliage.

J. Cover mechanics of arrangement (anchoring clay) with additional foliage.

K. If more material is needed to round out arrangement, give them some bits from your own supply.

L. Instruct them to use care, warn of possible dangers in carrying them home.

M. At this point, your work is finished but you should make your workroom available, if necessary, to any pupils why have not yet completed their arrangements.

## Questions Most Often Asked by Pupils

Q. *Why do some of my flowers have brown centers when they come out of the sand?*

A. There was some hidden moisture in the flower before it was put in the sand. Give questionable flowers the "sure-fire" test (Chapter VIII), and this won't happen.

Q. *I dried an aster and most of the petals fell off. Why?*

A. Asters have very little natural adhesive, but if you process the flower as soon as it has reached the stage of full bloom, this is less likely to happen. Even then use care in uncovering the flower and reinforce the petals. This is true of the daisy family, also.

Q. *Why do the yellow centers of my daisies separate while in the sand?*

A. The shrinkage of the outer calyx enclosing the centers causes the separation. As soon as you uncover the flower and while the centers are still pliable, gently work them back in place with the end of a toothpick, starting from the outer edge and working toward the center.

Q. *Why can't we do German iris?*

A. Because of the water content and extremely delicate structure of the petals which, upon close examination, look like tiny beads of frost, which is really moisture. After desiccation takes place the petals have the appearance of glass and a marked change in color takes place. I know of no way either to prevent this or correct it except chalking, which in this case doesn't prove to be very satisfactory.

Q. *I sprayed my flower after I chalked and dried it and it went streaked. Why?*

A.  You failed to remove the excess chalk before spraying and the spray loosened the excess and distributed it in streaks. Remove excess before spraying and this will not happen.

Q.  *Why do I have to wrap wire stems when they are already covered with green thread?*
A.  In the first place, the thread looks like thread and not like a stem, then too, the wire will not hold in the clay when you make the arrangement unless it is wrapped with floral tape.

Q.  *Why do white spots sometimes appear on my dark roses when I reinforce them with glue?*
A.  You did not put the glue where it belongs, which is in the center, not on the petals. Use greater care in applying it. If the center is difficult to reach, use a slender eyedropper to apply the glue or better yet, use Clear Glue, available at most hobby shops.

Q.  *Why do I have to take a large, full-blown rose apart to dry it? Why can't I dry it as I dry other large flowers?*
A.  Again, the natural glue seems to diminish in a full-blown rose and you are dealing with as many as forty or fifty petals in a Peace rose. When the flower is being uncovered, the action and pressure of the sand causes it to shatter, so you end up having to reglue them back anyhow. Why not do it correctly in the first place, thus eliminating all risk of breakage and distortion of petals?

Q.  *Why can't I glycerinize delicate greenery the same as coarser material?*
A.  I don't know why but you cannot. Whatever chemical action takes place is too severe for delicate textures. They either curl up or collapse, whereas heavy-textured greenery behaves beautifully.

Q.  *Why can't I shake a zinnia in the dye chalk bag, since it is a heavy-textured flower?*

A.  Part of the charm of a zinnia is its contrasting center, sparked with tiny yellow stars, which would be eliminated if it were colored the same as the petals. In addition, the chalk adheres too thickly to the rough-textured petals and has to be brushed off anyhow. Why not brush it on in the first place?

Q.  *I did some mock orange sprays and the flowers were flattened. Why?*
A.  You did not give enough attention to maintaining the contour. Do not attempt to cover a very large spray, but cut it in sections. Concentrate on each flower as the covering progresses. Keeping the sandbed level and equalizing the pressure, both inside and outside of the floret, will prevent this from happening.

Q.  *I preserved some pink peonies and they turned out fine but the dark red ones fell apart. Why?*
A.  Again, a difference in adhesive qualities between the two flowers. Process your red ones as soon as they come into full bloom. This will help.

Q.  *Why can't we do nasturtiums and geraniums?*
A.  Too much water content, therefore a radical change takes place in both color and texture. They look like darkened tissue paper when they come out of the sand. In addition, they are semitransparent. The pelargonium, Lady Washington, behaves better and is lovely.

Q.  *What about dinner-plate-size hibiscus?*
A.  Don't try them. The tremendous size and their finely ribbed texture causes them to break at the slightest movement. I doubt whether you could even get them out of the sand intact. I cannot.

Q.  *How can I preserve pussy willows?*
A.  Just cut them and use them.

Q. (From California): *When I do poinsettias, the sand clings to the centers and I can't get it off. Why is this?*

A. Another inconsistency of Mother Nature's. Sometimes she uses her glue too sparingly; other times, she uses an overabundance. In this case, the centers literally "cry glue." Wipe off the excess with a dab of cotton that has been saturated with vinegar. Dry carefully and process. This will help.

Q. *Why can't I do gladioli in the complete stalk instead of the individual flowers?*

A. The gladiolus is a difficult flower to do properly. You will have all you can do to process one flower and maintain its grace and form. If you tried to process the entire stalk at one time, its contour would be lost by distortion.

Q. *Why is sand better than silica gel for drying flowers?*

A. Read Chapters III and IV for full answer.

Q. *Some of the foliage in an arrangement that I made has turned white. What can I do about it?*

A. Remove it and either paint it or spray it green. If you had done this before you made the arrangement the discoloration would not have happened.

Q. *My friend from Hawaii sent me some flowers. I preserved them but was disappointed when they turned brown. Why?*

A. Stay away from most tropicals, too much water content.

Q. *Can I preserve funeral flowers?*

A. I don't advise it. They have probably been sprayed with water, moved and handled too many times, are probably bruised and by the time the service is over, beginning to wither.

Q. *Can I preserve bridal bouquets?*

A. No, for the same reasons. Add to them the throwing of the bouquet and you have your answer.

Q. *What about the dyes on the market which are supposed to dye the flowers by absorption through the stems?*

A. I have tried them and found them unsatisfactory by my standards.

Q. *The pins that I put in the stems of my fruit blossoms came out. What can I do?*

A. Don't worry. The holes made by the pins are still there. Insert another pin with glue.

Q. *Why do large chrysanthemums shatter and turn dark at the center?*

A. The great amount of water content in the large heavy varieties causes them to turn dark before complete desiccation can take place. Not enough adhesive on the petals causes them to shatter. Make sure that the flower is perfectly dry to begin with. Try reinforcing petals, *while the flower is fresh,* with all purpose Clear Glue, rather than diluted glue. The former does not darken the petals, the latter might. Let the glue dry *thoroughly* and process. Give extra heat to hasten the drying by placing the container in front of a heat register or in a warm sunny window.

# CHAPTER XVIII

# Encyclopedia of Flowers and Their Special Treatment

In the preceding chapters I have given instructions for treatment of flowers in general. Now let us consider each individual bloom and its specific problems.

We should always remember that all flowers have personalities. Every gardener knows this. The Oriental mystic recognizes it and endows a flower not only with a soul, but also with a language he claims to understand. He even classifies flowers as a link in the chain of being that begins with the birds and butterflies, goes into the fairy world, and culminates in the archangel.

The acceptance or recognition of this theory is not necessary to our work. Yet a realization of the differences and dispositions of flowers is an asset in mastering the art of preserving blossoms.

If you would be successful with flowers, you must learn to estimate their water content, color stability, ability to withstand humidity after they are dried, etc. If you are careful, you will soon learn which ones you can preserve and which to avoid. This may prove to be a heartbreaking experience for, as I have learned the hard way, you may find your favorites among the impossibles. You may console yourself with the thought they are not necessarily "lost souls," but simply call for more experimentation and research. Indeed, I have successfully coaxed quite a few stubborn ones to yield.

During the eighteen years of my work, I have preserved, with varying success, over two hundred kinds of cultivated flowers and their foliage, along with about seventy-five wild varieties. The following chart lists most of the cultivated flowers alphabetically, their requirements for being preserved, and what problems, if any, you might encounter in handling them. The wild varieties and foliage are treated individually in their respective chapters in the book.

### Specific Drying Time for Sand Only

It must be remembered that the time listed for each kind applies only to spring, summer and fall, and is for dry or average climates. Allow a little more time for humid areas. The directions and drying time are indicated for the sand treatment only.

If using silica gel, follow drying time indicated on the package. In general it requires about one week.

If using borax and cornmeal, a fairly safe rule to follow is to use one-half the time indicated for sand. But if using a mixture of sand and borax only, allow a couple of days less than for the borax and cornmeal method.

### Nomenclature

I have tried to list each specimen by its most popular name. The botanical is the most familiar in some cases, the common in others.

### Characteristics and Treatment of Individual Flowers

*Acacia*—Hang and dry. Natural grace of flower clusters can be restored by steaming over a tea kettle after spray is dried.

*Achimenes*—Face up; two weeks in sand. Process individual flowers. They may be brushed with powdered chalk if desired.

*African violet*—Face up; two weeks in sand. Singles, lavenders and purples are fine. Purples are improved if chalked before processing.

*Ageratum*—Face up; two weeks in sand. More than one cluster to a container is possible.

*Ajuga*—Face down; two weeks in sand. A ground-covering or rock garden plant which has both flowers and foliage that are valuable for drying.

*Allium*—Face up; two weeks in sand. No special problems.

*Almond* (flowering)—Horizontal; two weeks in sand. More than one spray to a container if container is wide enough, but each spray must be supported by cardboard props.

*Amaranth*—There are many kinds, some of which are grown for their brilliant foliage. In such cases cut the entire plant in sections and dry each section face up; two weeks in sand. Others have a tassel-like flower, some green, others red. In this case, strip off the foliage and dry only the tassels with a portion of stem attached, horizontal, two weeks in sand. Globe amaranth is the same as Gomphrena which is an "everlasting" and is best treated by hang and dry method.

*Amaryllis*—Face up; three weeks in sand. Great water content causes color to change. Process individual flowers. Brush on chalk while fresh to improve and preserve color. Spray for humidity.

*Anemone*—Face up; two weeks in sand. Stamens need reinforcing after drying with diluted glue if flower is double.

*Anthurium*—Face up; four weeks in sand. One of the tropicals that changes in color; turns brown but is valuable for a wood-toned arrangement.

*Apple blossom* (also crabapple, peach, cherry, plum, quince and other fruit blossoms)—Face up; two weeks in sand. Cut individual clusters, including accompanying foliage from branch. Insert pin in end of stem so that cluster can later be glued into place on original branch. Clusters may also be used singly in arrangements.

*Arabis*—Horizontal or face up; two weeks in sand.

*Aster*—Face up; two weeks in sand. Must be uncovered very carefully to prevent shattering. Must be thoroughly glued (with diluted glue) from bottom and top before handling or cleaning.

*Astilbe*—Either face up or face down; two weeks in sand. May be chalked if desired.

*Aubrietia*—Face up; two weeks in sand. More than one spray may be processed in one container.

*Azalea*—Face up; two weeks in sand. Accompanying foliage may be left on flower stem. Expect some drastic changes of color in the flame and red varieties. Pinks and whites are excellent. Foliage on stems may be brush painted when dry. Do not advise using chalk on flowers.

*Baby blue-eyes*—Face up; two weeks in sand. Can be used singly or in clusters for miniature arrangements.

*Baby's breath*—Hang and dry; about one week. May be dyed any color, either before or after drying. Use liquid dye.

*Bachelor's button*—Face up; special handling. More than one flower can be dried in a container. While flowers are fresh, glue "petals" from underneath by letting liquid glue drip through base. Then cut off all stem, leaving only the plump cuplike bracts. Pierce end of cup with toothpick, making a generous hole into which stem or wire may be inserted when flower is dry.

Flowers may be placed on plate in refrigerator to crisp while drying takes place. Use no water. Mix a generous amount of powdered chalk (dark blue with a little lavender) to color the sand. (About eight pounds of sand should be colored and can be used year after year for this purpose.) Select a shallow pan. Put the usual one inch of colored sand in the bottom. Place the bachelor's buttons face up in rows. Flowers should have about an inch of space on all sides. Cover with more colored sand and set pan in oven at 150° for two hours. When cool, uncover and insert wires or dried stems into flowers with glue. They may be put back on original stems if desired. (In this case, dry the branches of plant first, including foliage and stems. Cut branch of plant and dust with green powdered chalk. Give horizontal sand treatment. Be careful to keep stems well separated as you cover with sand.) Very good result—well worth all the trouble. The reason for the colored chalk and quick drying is that the flowers have a tendency to turn white if subjected to the two-week drying time, just as they sometimes do in the garden.

*Balsam*—Face up; two weeks in sand. Use individual blooms in miniature arrangements.

*Basket-of-gold*—Face up (short stems); horizontal (long stems); two weeks in sand. Reinforce color by sifting yellow powdered chalk on flower clusters while fresh.

*Beauty bush*—Horizontal; two weeks in sand. Somewhat difficult to clean when dry because sand sticks to hairy stems. Brush stems with baby talcum powder before processing to prevent this. Tertiary butyl alcohol solution may be used for drying if you prefer. (See Chapter III, "Methods Of Preserving Flowers".)

*Begonia*—(tuberous)—Face up; two weeks in sand. Great water content. All colors turn tan. Form preserves beautifully but I know of nothing that will preserve the color.

*Bellflower*—Face up; two weeks in sand. Whites preserve beautifully, blues turn white after several months. Brush with powdered chalk while fresh.

*Bells of Ireland*—Face down or horizontal; two weeks in sand. Use tall container plus collar if stalks are very tall. Give green dye bath before drying. Add a dab of glue to joint of each bell after it is dry.

*Blackberry lily*—Face up; two weeks in sand. Nice for miniature arrangements.

*Black-eyed Susan*—Face up; two weeks in sand. Brush each petal with powdered chalk while fresh. Should be reinforced from top center with diluted glue when dry.

*Bleeding heart*—Horizontal; two weeks in sand. Anchor the spray lightly in sand so that the open end of each heart is facing up. Gently fill each open heart with sand, then cover the whole spray. This is done to prevent the heart from flattening. Grace and beauty of form are perfectly preserved but you can expect a dark color if dry medium is used. Tertiary butyl alcohol solution preserves color perfectly. (See Chapter III, "Methods of Preserving Flowers.")

*Bluebell* (California)—Face up; two weeks in sand. Bells of cultivated plant larger than wild variety. Delightful little flower used in clusters in arrangements. I like to dust them with blue powdered chalk before drying. Use brush.

*Bluebell* (Virginia)—Face up; two weeks in sand. The same species as the wild ones but brought under cultivation. Do not remove flowers from branch. Process in position best suited to permit filling of tiny bells with sand. This will depend on the position individual florets assume. Do not chalk florets or you will destroy the pink and blue color effect.

*Bougainvillea*—Face up; two weeks in sand. Process complete flower cluster. If reinforcement of color is desired, use liquid dye. May be put back on original stem.

*Bridal wreath*—Horizontal; one week in sand. Dries beautifully but care should be taken to keep spray in curved, natural position. Cover each group of flowers, one at a time, working from both inside and outside of group until covered.

*Buttercup* (creeping)—Common name for the genus Ranunculus. Face up; ten days in sand. One of the best little flowers for drying. Use as many in container as desired, but avoid crowding. One of the few yellows that does not require color reinforcement. Use singly or in clusters in arrangement.

*Butterfly bush*—Face down; ten days in sand. I grow the white kind because it takes any color beautifully. Shake in chalk bag while fresh.

*Calendula*—Face up; two weeks in sand. The pot marigold is one yellow or orange flower that should not be dyed. During drying, it takes on a silky texture that is charming but which is destroyed by dyeing. May need reinforcing with diluted glue from top when dry.

*California poppy*—Same treatment as for wild variety. (See Chapter XIV, "Wild Material.")

*Calla lily*—Face up; two weeks in sand. Dries beautifully.

*Camellia*—Face up; two weeks in sand. A tricky one to do. I had some shipped to me in Utah and I processed them immediately upon arrival. The Pink Perfection came out beautifully, perhaps the truest pink flower I have done to date. The whites came out snowy white, but after a few months turned a pinkish tan and later a pure pink, their final color. The reds turned very much darker than when fresh. The new hybrid pinks turned purple.

I am convinced that more research and experiment must be done with this flower before it can be considered completely conquered.

*Campanula*—Face up; three weeks in sand. Individual bells should be cut from their stalks and processed. They can be used as individual specimens or replaced on the mother stalk. The whites and pinks dry beautifully but the blues turn white after several months.

*Candytuft*—Face up; two weeks in sand.

*Canna*—Face up; three weeks in sand. Cut individual flowers from stalk. Brushing with powdered chalk keeps them from turning transparent. The leaves should be dried separately as they are invaluable for certain types of arrangements.

*Canterbury bells*—Face up; three weeks in sand. Process as for Campanula.

*Carnation*—Face up; two weeks in sand. Petals rattle around in the dried flower because of shrinkage of the petal fibers, which run down through the elongated calyx. To correct this, separate the petals slightly and hold them apart at the top of the dried flower while you let a generous amount of diluted glue drip down through them to the calyx.
Tip the flower in every direction in order to make sure the glue is evenly distributed inside the calyx. Hold in this position for a few minutes until dry.

*Catalpa*—Face up; two weeks in sand. This lovely flower resembles a miniature orchid, but each flower must be separated from the large cluster for processing. Catalpas are lovely with ferns.

*Cereus* (night blooming)—Until now has resisted all of my attempts to dry it.

*Christmas Rose*—Face up; two weeks in sand.

*Chrysanthemum*—Face up; four weeks in sand. Uncover all varieties carefully to prevent shattering.

Pompoms and cushion mums must be reinforced with diluted glue when dry. Larger varieties present a problem not yet entirely solved. The water content is so great, the drying so slow, and the petals so heavy that flowers invariably shatter when being uncovered. They clearly demand a different kind of glue. It should be a quick-spreading type that will sink into the petal base and rapidly cover the entire base area. This requires a lot of glue but one that will not injure the petals themselves. Injury means discoloring in this case. Clear acetate cement is not satisfactory. It cannot be controlled and discolors the petals. A glue that I found in a hobby shop this summer, called Clear Glue, may be the answer. It is quick-spreading and does not turn the petals dark. I have not had the time to try it on chrysanthemums yet. I suggest the reader try it.

The basement is usually too cool during chrysanthemum days, so move the container to a warmer place; thus you may be able to cut the drying time to three weeks.

*Cineraria*—Face up; two weeks in sand. If petals are loose when uncovered, reinforce with diluted glue.

*Clarkia*—Face up or horizontal; two weeks in sand.

*Clematis*—Face down; three weeks in sand. Retains velvety texture if brushed with powdered chalk before drying.

To process, cut individual flowers; omit pin because stems are too thin to permit insertion. Form small mound of sand. Make small indentation in center with tip of finger. Into this put the bunched stamens. If tip of petals flair down, mound up sand underneath them before covering flower. Cover as directed. Mother vine holding leaves must be given the sand treatment. When flowers are dry, glue (undiluted) flowers back on and hold in place until glue is set. Spray for humidity.

*Cleome*—Face up; two weeks in sand.

*Cockscomb*—Hang and dry. If sand treatment is used, it becomes very difficult to remove the grains without injury to the fuzzy flower clusters. But even the hang and dry method will leave the cluster stiff and matted. This can be overcome by holding it over the spout of a boiling teakettle. Let the steam pass quickly over the flower cluster as you turn it in all directions. Almost immediately the cluster will fluff up and regain its grace and natural form. Hold it in the desired position for about a minute and it will become perfectly dry again.

*Columbine*—Face up; two weeks in sand. Do not process flowers that are too old; they tend to shatter. Baby talcum powder dusted inside each spur with a fine brush before processing makes cleaning easier. If segments of flower fall when dry, glue back on with undiluted glue.

*Coral bells*—Face down; two weeks in sand. Color may be enhanced with liquid dye bath.

*Coreopsis*—Face up; two weeks in sand. Should be dusted with powdered chalk to stabilize color before processing.

*Cosmos*—Face down; two weeks in sand. Make small mound of sand and indent in center with end of finger. Place yellow center of flower in this indentation and cover.

*Crape Myrtle*—Face up; ten days in sand. Individual flowers must be dried and later glued (undiluted) back on stem. Individual flowers may be used in miniature arrangements.

*Crocus*—Face up; three weeks in sand. Spray for humidity.

*Cup-flower*—Face up; two weeks in sand. Brush with powdered chalk before drying.

*Cupid's dart*—A strawlike flower but it is still better to process it face up, one week in sand.

*Cyclamen*—Face up; two weeks in sand. Pink kinds excellent.

*Daffodil*—Face up; three weeks in sand. Reinforce color with powdered chalk before drying. Spray for humidity.

*Dahlia*—Face up; two weeks in sand. Make mound of sand. Place stem in center to make covering of lower petals easier. Takes both liquid and chalk dye nicely. All behave well except dinner-plate size, which usually shatter because of great weight.

*Daisy*—Face up or face down; two weeks in sand. Singles best done face down. Make small mound of sand. Make small indentation with end of finger. Place yellow center over indentation and cover.

Marconi and fluffy doubles must be done face up. If yellow centers have separated when flower is removed from sand, press gently together with toothpick. Do this immediately, while centers are pliable. Singles may require reinforcement with glue (diluted) from center.

*Daisy* (Michaelmas)—Face up; two weeks in sand. Entire spray—leaves, flowers and buds—can be processed. The larger the container, the larger the spray can be. Each flower should receive a few drops of diluted glue after it is dry.

*Day lily*—Face up; three weeks in sand. Yellows are particularly successful. Both types of dye work well on fresh flower. Spray for humidity.

*Delphinium*—Horizontal and face down; two weeks in sand. Process long stalks in horizontal position. (See Chapter IX, "Covering the Flower.") Small laterals, Belladonna and Chinese kinds may be processed face down. Do not dye.

*Deutzia*—Horizontal; two weeks in sand. Dust thoroughly with baby talcum powder before drying. Responds better to tertiary butyl alcohol treatment than to sand. (See Chapter III, "Methods of Preserving Flowers.")

*Dianthus* (pinks)—Face up; two weeks in sand. Treatment same as for carnations.

*Doronicum*—Face up or face down; three weeks in sand. If cup shape is desired, cover face down. Otherwise cover face up. (See Chapter IX, "Covering the Flower.") Requires glueing (diluted) through center when dry. Slow to fade so dyeing is optional.

*Eglantine* (sweetbrier)—Face up; two weeks in sand. I cannot praise this flower too highly. It is a little gem when dried. Cut individual flowers, process and apply to original branch which has been previously dried. No chalking. Advise adding a drop of flower (rose) perfume to heart of flower when dry.

*English daisy*—Face up; two weeks in sand. More than one can be processed in same container if flowers are small.

*False dragonhead*—Face up or face down; two weeks in sand. If bells point downward, process face down; if they point straight out or slightly upward, as sometimes happens, process face up.

*Feverfew*—Face down; two weeks in sand. Entire spray of flowers may be done at one time, but avoid crowding. Process delicate foliage on sprays as well as the flowers; this gives them a natural fresh look. The foliage must be painted green after the spray has been dried. Touch centers of flowers with yellow chalk.

*Flax*—One of the untouchables. Its petals fall when uncovered. I do not consider it worth the trouble to glue them back on.

*Forget-me-not*—Face up; two weeks in sand. Lovely, but don't cut too many at a time, for they wither very quickly after being cut. As many as container will hold may be processed, provided they don't touch one another or the container. I like the early spring forget-me-nots best.

*Forsythia*—Face up or face down, according to the direction the bells take; two weeks in sand. Best to cut spray in sections and process individually.

*Foxglove*—Face up; two weeks in sand. Cut bells from mother stem and process individually. After they are dry, glue back on mother stem. Spray for humidity.

*Fritillaria*—Face up; two weeks in sand. Do not chalk as this hides their beautiful markings.

*Fuchsia*—Face up; three weeks in sand. All varieties do well but I like to brush them in powdered chalk before processing to intensify their striking coloring.

*Gaillardia*—Face up; two weeks in sand. No special problems.

*Gazania*—Face up; two weeks in sand. Do not chalk. Part of their beauty is in their silky sheen which would be destroyed if chalk were used. Spray for humidity.

*Geranium*—Face up; two weeks in sand. Try them if you must. The cultivated ones are very disappointing. They shatter and petals go paper thin. Of course they can be chalked and petals glued back on, if you insist. The pelargoniums are best for preserving. Try some of them, particularly Lady Washington. Wild true geranium is excellent.

*Gerbera* (Transvaal daisies)—Face up; two weeks in sand. Reinforce petals when dry.

*Geum*—Face up; two weeks in sand. Expect red variety to turn quite dark.

*Gladiolus*—Face up; two weeks in sand. Cut and process individual flowers. Add pins before processing and when dry, glue and replace flowers on preserved stem. Or they may be used singly in arrangements, which is the way I like to use them. They must be dusted with chalk before and after they are dried. Spray for humidity.

*Globeflower* (Trollius)—Face down; two weeks in sand. Color fades unless reinforced.

*Globe thistle*—Face up; two weeks in sand. Reinforce with diluted glue after drying. Chalking helps to retain the color.

*Gloriosa daisy*—Face up; two weeks in sand. Petals may need reinforcing when dry.

*Glory-of-the-snow* (Chionodoxa)—Face up; two weeks in sand.

*Gloxinia*—Face up; two weeks in sand. Hot house varieties unsuccessful; hardy varieties better.

*Godetia*—Face up; two weeks in sand. Especially lovely, it takes on satin sheen.

*Golden chain*—Horizontal; two weeks in sand. Reinforce color before processing.

*Golden glow*—Face up; two weeks in sand. Reinforce color before processing.

*Golden rain*—Two weeks in sand. Using any one of the three methods best suited to the spray and container. Reinforce color before processing.

*Gomphrena*—Hang and dry.

*Grape hyacinth*—Complete failure.

*Hawthorn*—Horizontal; two weeks in sand. Foliage and flowers can be left intact on spray while it is being processed.

*Heather*—Hang and dry or stand upright until crisp. Spray with clear plastic spray to prevent shattering.

*Helianthemum* (Rockrose)—Face up; two weeks in sand.

*Hen-and-chickens*—Face up. Takes months to dry then turns white and paper thin.

*Hibiscus*—Face up; three weeks in sand. Medium sizes very nice, but I do not advise drying extremely large flowers. They break easily.

*Hollyhock*—Face up; two weeks in sand. Excellent results. Try some of the powder puffs. To paint calyx and thin green stem properly, use extra amount of turpentine in green paint. Touch calyx with brush and let the thin paint flow over surface.

*Honesty*—Hang and dry until crisp. Remove outer shells or pods when dry.

*Honeysuckle*—Face up; two weeks in sand.

*Horse chestnut*—Face up; three weeks in sand. Dust with baby talcum powder before processing to neutralize stickiness.

*Hyacinth*—Face up; three weeks in sand. Turns somewhat transparent due to large water content. Try painting with Flower Sculture Formula. (See Chapter XV, "Flower Sculpture.")

*Hydrangea*—Face up; two weeks in sand. Takes liquid dye, resents chalk. Green ones are especially good.

*Hypericum*—Face up; two weeks in sand.

*Impatiens*—Face up; two weeks in sand. May be dusted with chalk.

*Iris*—Face up; three weeks in sand. Dutch iris very good, but the German iris become transparent when dried.

*Jonquil*—Face up; three weeks in sand. Brush with chalk when fresh. Spray for humidity.

*Kerria*—Horizontal; two weeks in sand. Process sprays, leaves, flowers and all.

*Lace flower* (Blue)—Face down; two weeks in sand. Let sand flow close to central stem. This preserves umbrella shape. May be chalked while fresh.

*Larkspur*—Horizontal or face down; two weeks in sand. Process extra long sprays horizontally. You may put several sprays in container at same time. Support with cardboard tabs and do not crowd. Short sprays are done face down. Use no chalk. They dry true to color and do not fade.

*Lavender*—Face down; two weeks in sand. Turn dark purple when dried.

*Lewisia*—Face up; three weeks in sand. Use no chalk and spray for humidity when dried. Have had experience only with L. rediviva, with excellent results.

*Lilac*—Face up; two weeks in sand. No problems, but you may need help in handling a large container of sand, which a large cluster demands. A very satisfactory flower. May be chalked. Whites stay white longer if chalked before processing.

*Lily*—Face up; three weeks in sand. There are many problems in connection with lilies. Easter lilies are successful, but other white kinds may turn tannish. You can be success-ful with yellows and oranges, but they do eventually fade and flop. Spray for humidity as soon as taken out of the sand, then try coating them with Flower Sculpture Formula of the correct tint. (See Chapter XV on "Flower Sculture.")

*Lily, Water*—Face up; two weeks in sand. Water lilies are wonderful and dry beautifully, all colors. Never chalk the white ones as this destroys their pearly sheen. Other colors may be dusted with chalk if you so desire. The only problem with them is to get them perfectly *dry* before processing. I start with a series of brushes. When one becomes wet, I discard it and start with another dry one. Make sure both inside and outside of all petal surfaces are completely dry. Do not neglect the yellow center. When you are certain it is dry also, brush a bit of yellow chalk over its surface. Turn upside down and pat lightly to remove excess. Cover, maintaining oval curve of petals.

*Lily of the valley*—Horizontal or face down; two weeks in sand. Here is one that has eluded me for eighteen years. It is especially heartbreaking because it is one of my favorites. The sand method preserves the contour but they don't remain white; they turn a parchment color. Chalking does no good. The tertiary butyl alcohol treatment does pretty well but it leaves them so brittle and fragile that they cannot be handled without breakage. But I will not admit defeat, not permanently. Next year I shall dry some and then give them the Flower Sculpture Formula treatment, with a bit of white acrylic paint added to the formula. This might work. Of course stems must be painted light green when dry.

*Lobelia*—Face up; two weeks in sand. More than one to a container if desired.

*Locust* (black)—Face down; two weeks in sand. May be chalked if desired.

*Love-in-a-mist*—Face up; two weeks in sand.

*Lythrum*—Face down; two weeks in sand. Drastic change in color: pinks turn lavender.

*Magnolia*—Face up; two weeks in sand. Have tried only M. soulangeana, which turned brown. The foliage is excellent, however.

*Marguerite*—Face up; two weeks in sand. Process as for single daisies.

*Marigold*—Face up; two weeks in sand. Readers of my previous book may wonder why I now do this flower face up instead of face down. Through steady comparisons, I have found the face-up method to be the best. But a smooth high volcano-like mound must be prepared. Into the tip of this insert the short stem. This leaves the lower petals free and capable of being covered without distortion. Build high mound of sand all around the inside of the container, tip gently toward the flower, on all four sides, letting the sand flow into the petals without disturbing them. Repeat until covered. In this way the fluffiness of the top is maintained which would be crushed if done face down. The petals may require gluing (diluted) from underneath at base of petals.

*Mock orange*—Face up; ten days in sand. One of the finest white flowers grown. Process individual clusters with accompanying foliage, which may be stained with green dye or painted with green paint after flower has dried. Clusters may be used as individual specimens, or returned to original mother stem.

*Morning glory*—Face up; two weeks in sand, if tried. Will flop and the color changes drastically.

*Moss rose*—Face up; two weeks in sand. What a pity more people don't grow it! The beauty lies in the moss-like covering of stem and calyx. This moss is very sticky, and any dry desiccant clings to it heavily, making it impossible to clean without destroying the moss. Tertiary butyl alcohol solution No. 1 suits it best and does not destroy the moss. (See Chapter III, "Methods of Preserving Flowers.")

After it dries, paint moss with green stem paint, but dilute with extra turpentine to the point where your paint is very thin. Dip the brush in the paint and then just touch the moss. The paint will spread rapidly through the filaments, restoring its natural look and will not destroy the moss.

Process only buds and partially opened flowers and you will be delighted if you combine them with forget-me-nots.

*Narcissus*—Face up; two weeks in sand. Spray for humidity.

*Nasturtium*—Face up; two weeks in sand. Not very successful. They change in color, and petals become thin and semi-transparent.

*Oleander*—Face up; two weeks in sand. Whites are especially fine if dusted lightly with white powdered chalk before processing.

*Onions* (ornamental)—Face up; two weeks in sand. Process entire flower cluster.

*Orchid*—Face up; four weeks in sand. Flower must be perfectly fresh and not bruised. Most kinds have a tendency to turn slightly brown at base of petals. Cattleya mossiae gives best results. Cypripediums tend to turn brown. Suggest you try tertiary butyl alcohol solution. (See Chapter III, "Methods of Preserving Flowers.")

*Oregon grape*—Face up; two weeks in sand. Cut and process flower clusters.

*Painted daisy*—Face up; two weeks in sand. A beautiful subject to preserve. Colors are more brilliant in preserved flower than in fresh. Treatment same as for daisies.

*Encyclopedia of Flowers and Their Special Treatment*

*Pansy*—Horizontal if long-stemmed; face up if short-stemmed; three weeks in sand. Cut flowers with stems as long as possible, and leave stems on. Spray for humidity after dried.

*Passionflower*—Face up; two weeks in sand.

*Pentstemon*—Face down; two weeks in sand. The wild variety is one of the very best blue flowers.

*Peony*—Face up; two weeks in sand. One of the best flowers for preserving. Single and tree peonies are very successful; also pure whites and pinks of double form. Double reds sometimes shatter. Preserve as soon as flower comes into full bloom. Remove from sand carefully.

*Petunia*—Face up; three weeks in sand. Dust stems, calyx and underflowers—but never face of flower—with baby talcum powder. This is done to help keep the sand from coating sticky surfaces. Even then they must be cleaned carefully. Stay away from reds. Some pinks turn lavender. Whites are lovely.

*Phlox*—Face down; three weeks in sand. If the cluster is not too large it can be done in its entirety. But phlox usually requires brushing with chalk to retain its original color. This is very difficult to do satisfactorily with the flower head intact. I have found that it is easier and better to remove the florets, dust them and process them face down and then glue them back on. You end up with a fresher looking flower and not any more work in the long run.

*Poinsettia*—Face up; three weeks in sand. Remove excess natural glue or sticky substance from stamens and pistil with cotton dampened with vinegar. Dry thoroughly and process. A dusting with powdered chalk of same color, either before or after drying, restores natural color and velvety texture. A petal or two may fall when being uncovered. They can be glued back easily with undiluted glue.

‡‡  194  ‡‡

*Poppy* (California)—Face up; two weeks in sand. Yellow and orange colors turn white very soon after drying. They resent dyeing. Try coating of Flower Sculpture Formula, correctly colored. (See Chapter XV, "Flower Sculture.") Red shade turns a golden brown.

*Poppy* (Oriental)—Face up; two weeks in sand. Only partially successful. Petals fall and must be glued back on. Color changes drastically. Flower flops at the slightest increase in humidity after drying.

*Portulaca*—Face up; three weeks in sand. Another one brought into the fold. For many years I tried to preserve this little beauty, without success. Now it is quite easy. Just powder it well with baby talcum powder before processing. It behaves like an angel.

*Primrose*—Face up; two weeks in sand.

*Prince's-feather*—Horizontal; two weeks in sand. Process long clusters without leaves. Dusting with properly colored chalk before processing improves color. Cut before seeds form. Very effective if used for drooping lines in arrangement.

*Ranunculus*—Face up; two weeks in sand. Spray for humidity.

*Red-hot poker*—Can't be done. It shatters.

*Rhododendron*—Face up; two weeks in sand. Process individual flowers. They may be replaced on mother stem later if desired. Flowers fade rather quickly so a brushing with powdered chalk is recommended before processing. Spray for humidity.

*Rose* (buds and half-blown)— Face up; two weeks in sand. This includes every phase of bloom from bud to two-thirds open. It also includes every kind and class from the first teas, floribundas, ramblers, grandifloras to miniatures, bedding shrubs and climbers.

Some change color more than others. Singles probably will need reinforcing with diluted glue from top center. All will give a good account of themselves if properly done.

The complete cluster of polyantha may be processed at one time. Yellows need dusting with chalk to prevent fading. Other colors may be chalked with the exception of the dark reds.

*Rose* (full-blown)—Full-blown hybrid teas of specimen size require a different treatment from that given buds or flowers in partial bloom. Because of size, weight, and fragility, they often shatter. To preserve them properly and perfectly, proceed as follows:

Have ready a rather large container, and put about one inch of sand in the bottom. Remove petals, one at a time, until flower is completely stripped except for calyx and stamens. Do this carefully so that you don't tear the petals. It is best to twist them off at their bases. Stand them upright in rows in the sand, allowing about one inch of space between each petal and each row. The very small irregular ones may simply be laid on the sand. Cover with sand, being careful to keep the petals straight up until process is completed. In separate container cover stem holding calyx and stamens. Allow to dry in sand two weeks. Then uncover slowly, removing petals one at a time as you go. Do not attempt to pull them out of the sand. Uncover stem with calyx.

Assemble, clean and sort petals according to size. You will need some toothpicks and clear acetate cement. Use undiluted glue only. Using a toothpick, spread a thin coating of glue on top of the calyx and as close to the stamens as possible. While you are gluing, be careful at all times to hold the stem in the left hand, stamens pointed downward, until dry. Also, keep the petals as close to stamens as possible, no matter how many there are to be assembled.

Start with the smallest petals first. Dip end of each in glue, and place at base of stamens where glue was first applied. Encircle stamens with a sparse row of petals equal or nearly equal in size, and leave a small space between each.

Hold the flower, pointed downward, for about a minute to let glue set. Now glue on a second slightly larger row in the same manner, placing new petals in spaces between those already in place. Again allow to dry. Now glue on a third row of next size. This time, place each petal so that it overlaps the previous one, exactly as they grew on the rose.

At no time do you place a petal directly behind another. Overlap and stagger them. Each row should receive one or two more petals than the preceding row until the maximum size of the flower has been reached. Do not use too much glue or the petals will slide off. This will also happen if you do not allow enough time for preceding rows to dry before applying new ones. Try to keep petals forward as close to center as possible without distortion. Complete entire flower and allow to remain in face-down position until completely dry.

This operation may sound frighteningly difficult, but it isn't. The entire reassembling of a large rose can be done in about half an hour. And I know of no other way to accomplish it. Waiting for each row of petals to dry is time-wasting, but you can put three or four flowers together in the same amount of time that it takes to do one. Proceed as follows: when the first row of petals on a flower is in place, snap a clothespin around the stem and set it on the edge of a table with a weight to hold it, letting the flower hang free (face down) until glue is set. In the meantime, proceed with a second and third flower. By the time the last flower is completed, the first one will be dry and ready for its second row of petals. You can even watch television while you are working.

When the flower is perfectly dry, turn it over and examine it. You may notice some finger marks here and there. These can be removed by pressing lightly in back of the petal where they occur. They will disappear immediately, and the smooth petal will spring back into place.

For assembling original stem and foliage, see Chapter XI, "How to Prepare Stems."

*Rose acacia*—Face down; two weeks in sand.

*Rose of Sharon*—Face up; four weeks in sand. Spray for humidity.

*Sage* (scarlet)—Face down; two weeks in sand. Darkens somewhat. Be sure to pop open the flowers so that the sand can get in.

*Salpiglossis*—Face up; two weeks in sand.

*Scabiosa*—Face up; two weeks in sand. Must be reinforced with diluted glue through the center.

*Schizanthus*—Face up; two weeks in sand. Flower fades and becomes transparent.

*Scillia*—Face down; three weeks in sand. One of the most beautiful blue flowers in the garden, and they stay blue. But the seed pod continues to form and develop while they are in the sand. When you take them out the enlarged centers are too heavy for the flower, so consequently weight it down. Oh, the tricks Mother Nature plays on us.

*Sedum*—Hang and dry. Flower head can be dyed with liquid dye while fresh or after dried.

*Silver-lace vine*—Horizontal; two weeks in sand. Good trailing effects. May be dyed.

*Smoke tree*—Cut feathery blooms and stand upright in container until dry. May be chalked if desired. Foliage excellent dried in clumps.

*Snapdragon*—Face up; two weeks in sand.

*Snowball*—Face up; two weeks in sand. Especially good if processed while green.

*Snowdrop*—Face up; two weeks in sand.

*Spiraea*—Horizontal or face down, according to the size of the spray; two weeks in sand. May be chalked while fresh if desired. Shake spray in chalk bag.

*Stock*—Face down; two weeks in sand. Process entire stalk.

*Sweet alyssum*—Face up; ten days in sand. More than one flower to a container.

*Sweet pea*—Face up; two weeks in sand. Expect some color change and some transparency in pastels. But results are lovely just the same.

*Sweet pea* (perennial)—Face up; two weeks in sand. Cut entire cluster with long stem left on. Process in deep container.

*Sweet sultan*—Face up; two weeks in sand.

*Sweet William*—Face up; two weeks in sand. Process entire flower cluster.

*Tamarisk*—Set spray of shrub in empty can or container until dry. Spray with clear plastic spray to prevent shattering.

*Tigridia*—Face up; four weeks in sand. Not very satisfactory. It is too fragile to be cleaned successfully without damage. You might try dusting it with talcum powder before processing.

*Tradescantia*—Face up; three weeks in sand. Spray for humidity.

*Trumpet creeper* (common; also called trumpet vine)—Face up; two weeks in sand. Orange flowers turn golden brown. Process individual flowers for brown accent in arrangement.

*Tulip*—Face up; three weeks in sand. Some colors turn dark. Some petals may fall when being uncovered, but it is well worthwhile to glue (undiluted) them together. I used Flower Sculpture Formula on several colors this spring with excellent results. (See Chapter XV, "Flower Sculpture.")

*Unicorn plant*—Grown primarily for seed capsule which may be used either gilded or left natural.

*Verbena*—Face down; three weeks in sand.

*Veronica*—Horizontal or face down; two weeks in sand. All colors good except lavender-blue, which dulls in color.

*Viola*—Face up; three weeks in sand. Process as for pansy.

*Violet*—Face up or horizontal; two weeks in sand. Process V. odorata horizontally keeping long stem on. Process more than one to a container. Purple Showers (a hybrid) is excellent for drying because the flowers are larger. May be chalked while fresh.

*Water poppy*—Face up; two weeks in sand.

*Weigela*—Horizontal; two weeks in sand. Cleaning is difficult. Try brushing all green parts with baby talcum powder.

*Wisteria*—Face down; two weeks in sand. Not very satisfactory. Too much shrinkage.

*Yarrow*—Hang and dry. Same treatment as for wild variety. May be dyed (liquid). Spray with clear plastic spray to prevent shattering.

*Zinnia*—Face up; two weeks in sand. Brush petals with colored powdered chalk to restore velvety smoothness before or after drying.

# A Parting Word

And so we come to a turn in the road; the end for me and the beginning for you. It has been a gratifying experience for me to go this far with you.

The purpose of this effort has been to teach you to preserve growing things: plants from the garden, the mountain, the desert and elsewhere. A careful application of the rules that I have laid down, and a determination on your part to try, will accomplish just that. I hope that you will always strive for perfection. I would rather you learned to do ONE flower well than a room full of imperfect ones.

But I warn you. Your beds will go unmade, your dishes unwashed and probably your husband will go walking around with holes in his socks. You won't mind, however, and neither will he, when he sees the joy that this art has brought into your life.

In looking back, perhaps I can say that my greatest excitement was in watching my pupils uncover their first flower. I can see them now, with worried looks on their faces, and I can still hear their little squeals of delight and surprise as their first little gem was uncovered. They didn't think they could do it, but they found out that they could.

The most rewarding moments have been those when pupils confessed that in addition to acquiring the knowledge of flower drying, they had a new world opened up to them for the first time—the great out-of-doors. They had learned to SEE rather than just to LOOK.

So plant your gardens, prepare your sand, gather up your tools and start out on a new and wonderful adventure!

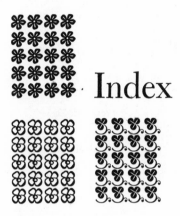

# Index

Acacia, 20–21, 50, 176
Acacia gum, 144–45, 150, 152
Acetate cement, 74, 80–81, 90, 92
Achillea, 103
Achimenes, 176
Acorns, 119
Acroclinium, 21
Activated Alumina, 25
African marigolds, 45, 85, 92
African violet, 176
Ageratum, 177
Aiken, George D., 116
Ajuga, 103, 177
Alexander the Great, 2
Allium, 177
Almond, 4, 177
Althaea, 104
Amaranth, 177
  globe, 21, 177, 188
Amaryllis, 177
American Crayon Company, 57
Ammobium, 21
Anemone, 49, 104, 177
Anthurium, 177
Apple blossom, 177–78
Arabis, 178
Artemesia, 104
Artichokes, 110
Asters, 49–51, 84–85, 127–28, 170, 178
Astilbe, 104, 178
Aubretia, 69, 178
Autumn leaves, 99
Azalea, 49, 51, 105, 178
Aztecs, 1–2

Baby blue-eyes, 178
Baby's breath, 20, 56, 112, 178
Bachelor's button, 49, 50, 54–55, 178–79
Balsam, 105, 128, 150, 179
Bark, 119
Basket-of-gold, 50, 179
Bay-salt, 3
Beech, 104
Begonia, 104, 179
Bellflower, 179
Bells of Ireland, 180
Berries, 119
Blackberry lily, 180
Black-eyed Susan, 128, 180
Bleeding heart, 26, 104, 180
  steershead, 140
Blue flowers, 49–50, 54–55, 109
  oolitic sand and, 24, 31
Bluebells, 70, 129, 180
Borage, 109
Borax, 18, 21–22, 66
  colors and, 22, 31, 75
  contour of flower in, 27–28
  dangers of, 10, 22
  drying time with, 22, 28, 75, 176
  petals affected by, 22, 28–30
  texture and, 32
Botany, 16, 114–15
Bougainvillea, 49, 180
Boxwood, 99, 119
Branches, 119
Bridal wreath, 45, 51, 105, 180–81
Broom, 105
Burpee Seed Company, 21

# Index

Buttercup, 50, 90
  creeping, 69, 181
Butterflies, 156–57
Butterfly bush, 104, 181

Cabbages, 108–9
Cactus, 49, 50, 61, 114, 116, 117, 123–27
  gathering of, 118–19, 123–25
Caladium, 104
Calendula, 181
Calla lily, 51, 181
Calyx, 67, 83, 85, 170
  paint for, 91, 92, 94, 161
Camellia, 50, 104, 105, 181
Campanula, 46, 182
Candying, 16, 109, 143–46
Candytuft, 49, 182
Canna, 104, 182
Canterbury bells, 45, 51, 182
Carnation, 45, 49, 69, 85, 182
  stems of, 90, 94–95
Carrot greens, 107
Castor bean, 104
Catalpa, 104, 182
Catkin, 129
Cattail, 20, 119, 129
Cedar, 105
Celosia, 20–21
Centers
  brown, 170, 174
  cleaning sand from, 173
  dyeing of, 60, 86, 128, 130, 172
  separation of, 85, 130, 170
Cereus, 182
Chalk, see Dyeing and painting
Cheat, 141
Cherry blossom, 177–78
Chicory, 129
Chives, 20, 56, 110–12
Choke cherry, 105, 121, 129
Christmas greens, 105
Christmas rose, 182
Chrysanthemum, 25, 49, 85, 105, 174, 182–83
Cineraria, 183
Clarkia, 183
Clear Glue, 171, 174, 183
Clematis, 45, 50, 70, 72, 121, 130, 183
  spray preserved of, 105, 130
Cleome, 183
Cloister and the Hearth, The, 3, 7
Clover, 130
Cockscomb, 49, 183–84
Cole, Elizabeth, 152, 156
Coleus, 104
Colorado Dye and Chemical Company, Inc., 99
Color, 30–31, 48–51
  bicarbonate of soda and, 37

blue, 24, 31, 49–50, 54–55, 109
  in cacti, 123, 127
  changes (fading) in, 6, 48–50, 115, 170, 172, 183
  in flower arrangements, 11, 154
  Flower Sculpture Formula and, 150–52
  of green plant tissue, 50, 99, 173
  in oolitic sand, 24, 31
  orange, 50, 53
  overdrying and, 22, 23, 75
  in restoration of old flowers, 161, 162
  with silica gel method, 23, 31
  stability of, 48, 175
  of stems, 91
  in tertiary butyl alcohol method, 26
  white, 22, 26, 46, 50–51, 57, 123
  See also Dyeing and painting; and specific flower
Columbine, 51, 104, 130, 184
Composites, 84–85
Conifer foliage, 99, 105
Containers, 39–44, 62–63, 66
  collars for, 43–44, 62, 72
  covering for, 75
  for foliage, 43–44, 101, 102
  for small flowers, 69
  for storage, 44
  storage of while drying, 68, 72–75
Coral bells, 104, 184
Coreopsis, 50, 184
Corn, 108
Cornmeal, 10, 18
  borax-and-cornmeal method with, 21–22, 27–28, 31, 32, 66, 75, 176
Cornstarch, 18
Corydalis brandgei, 104
Cosmos, 45, 49, 51, 70, 72, 184
Cotoneaster, 105
Crabapple blossom, 177–78
Crape myrtle, 49, 184
Creeping Jenny, 105
Crested wheat, 141
Crete, 2
Crocus, 46, 184
Croton, 104
Cup-flowers, 184
Cupid's dart, 184
Cyclamen, 49, 184

Daffodil, 46, 50, 150, 185
Dahlia, 49, 50, 69, 85, 185
  pink, 31
Daisies, 40, 45, 51, 60, 85–86, 170, 185
  English, 186
  Esther Read, 69
  gloriosa, 50, 188
  Michaelmas, 185

# Index

painted, 49, 193
stems from, 89
Transvaal, 187
wild, 130
Dandelion, 130
Day lily, 46, 185
Delbruck, Mel, 7
Delphinium, 23, 40, 45, 50, 61, 70–71, 121, 130–31, 185
  cutting of, 52
  foliage of, 104
  long sprays of, 74
Deutzia, 185
Dianthus (pinks), 90, 185
Dock, 20, 131
Dogtooth violet, 131
Doronicum, 50, 186
Dry Oasis, 169
Drying media (desiccants), 5, 18–26, *see also specific desiccants*
Drying time, 68, 75, 76, 174
  in borax methods, 22, 28, 75, 176
  climate affecting, 176
  for foliage, 101–6
  in oolitic sand method, 30
  in oven, 55, 179
  in silica gel method, 23, 28, 75, 176
  in tertiary butyl alcohol method, 26
  for vegetables, 109
  *See also specific plants*
Dusty miller, 100, 104
Dyeing and painting, 31, 49, 53–61, 65, 174
  of artichoke blooms, 110
  chalk method of, 51, 59–61, 84, 86, 170–72
  of chive flowers, 111–12
  for classroom use, 56, 122
  cleaning and, 54, 84
  of corn tassels, 108
  of flower centers, 60, 86, 128, 130, 172
  in flower shows, 16, 56
  of foliage, 15, 50, 54, 91, 99, 103–6, 123, 173, 193
  liquid method of, 56–57
  in restoration of old flowers, 161
  sheen and, 46, 61, 92, 123, 187, 191
  of stems, 90–92, 94, 168–69
  teachers' manual on, 165–66
  texture and, 49, 54, 86, 123, 134, 171–72
  transparency and, 170
  of wild flowers, 56, 119, 122–23
  *See also specific plants*

Eczema, 10
Eglantine, 105, 186
Egypt, 2

Elizabeth Cole, Inc., 152, 156
English daisy, 186
Euonymus, 106
Evening primrose, 46, 50, 122,
Evergreens, 12
Everlastings, 6, 21, 56, 137, 177

Fading, *see* Color; Dyeing and painting
False dragonhead, 50, 186
False Solomon's-seal, 131
Fan-Tail willow, 89
Ferns, 43, 87, 98, 99, 104, 182
  leather, 102–4
  maidenhair, 102–4, 127
Feverfew, 89, 103, 104, 186
Fir, 105
Fireweed, 132
Flaming Gorge Dam, 15–16, 115, 133
Flax, 186
Florida Engineering and Industrial Experiment Station, 25–26
Flower arranging, 11–15, 89, 153–63, 169
  anchoring for, 154, 169, 171
  containers for, 154, 156
  foliage in, 96, 154, 173
  fragrances for, 156
  under glass bells, 157–58
  of small flowers, 90
Flower preservation, 19, 175–76
  for beginners, 45, 63–65, 68, 116
  of bridal bouquets, 173
  care taken after, 6, 86–87, 157–62
  in classroom use, 16, 56, 114–15, 134
  cleaning in, 80–87, 160–62, 171
  climate and, 86, 176
  color in, *see* Color; Dyeing and painting
  containers for, *see* Containers
  contour in, 22, 27–28, 55, 68–69, 72, 150, 172
  covering in, 62–75, 165–66, 172
  cutting for, 51–52, 62, 65, 94–95, 117
  dry cleaning fluid for, 86–87
  drying in, 52, 57, 59, 65, 191
  as fine art, 7, 11
  flower selection in, 45–47, 66
  of funeral flowers, 173
  gardening and, 47–48, 116
  grooming in, 30, 85–86
  handling in, 77, 81
  hang and dry method of, 5–6, 11, 19–21, 56
  history of, 2–4, 19–20
  as hobby, 7–11
  in home decor, 8–9, 11–17
  inventory for, 62–63, 80, 90–91, 118–19, 164

light for, 63
moisture-proofing in, 55, 61, 84, 86, 122, 133, 151, 160, 169
moisture test in, 59, 170, 174
monetary potentials of, 11
for museums, 11, 15–16, 55, 115, 122–23, 134, 141–42
position of flower in, 66, 192
    face-down, 70–72, 79
    face-up, 66–69, 77
    faith method in, 71–72
    horizontal, 72–75, 79–80
by pressing, 16
questions about, 170–74
restoration of old flowers in, 160–62
schedule and, 47–48, 201
of small flowers, 69
special treatment in, 46–47, 175–200
of sprays, 43, 69–75, 92, 103, 105–6, 172, 173, 177
storage in, 44, 68, 72–75, 78–79, 86
teachers' manual on, 164–74
transportation of, 6, 158–60, 169
of tropical flowers, 173, 177
uncovering in, 76–80, 84–85, 170, 171
values of, 8–9
at varying stages of bloom, 68–69
*See also* Wild flowers and plants; *and specific plants; subjects*
Flower Preservations, Inc., 25, 84
Flower Sculpture Formula, 13, 16–17, 46, 150–52, 191, 195, 200
    preparation of, 150–52
    on wild flowers, 122, 128, 133, 137, 138, 141, 150
Flower shows, 16, 56
Flower trees, 15, 90
Flowering shrubs, 103
Foliage, 38, 65, 69, 89, 176
    with candied fruit, 150
    chalk dusting for, 54
    chart on, 103–6
    cleaning of, 87
    color preservation of, 50, 99, 173
    containers for, 43–44, 101, 102
    cutting of, 98
    drying time for, 101–6
    dyeing or painting of, 15, 50, 54, 91, 99, 103–6, 123, 173, 193
    flexibility in, 98, 99, 101
    in flower arranging, 96, 154, 173
    glycerinized, 14, 97–100, 102–6, 119, 171
    hang and dry method with, 21, 97, 100, 141
    ironing of, 97, 99–100
    plastic bag treatment for, 121–22, 128
    preservation of, 94, 97–106, 171

pressed, 97
sand-dried, 97, 99–106
skeletonizing of, 97, 100
steaming for, 21
talcum powder for, 128, 138, 140, 179, 194, 200
teachers' manual on, 167–68
of vegetables, 107–9
of wild plants, 119, 121–23
*See also specific plants*
Foliage trees, 90
Forget-me-nots, 69, 90, 132, 186
Forsythia, 187
Foxglove, 187
Fritillaria, 135, 187
Fruit, candied, 146–50
Fruit blossoms, 45, 49, 51, 66, 110, 174, 177–78
Fruit foliage, 99, 104
Funkia, 104
Fuschia, 49, 106, 187

Gaillardia, 187
Gardening, 47–48, 116, 175
Garzania, 187
Gentian, 50
    fringed, 132
Geranium, 132, 172, 187
Gerbera, 187
Geum, 187
Gilia, 121, 132–33
Gladiolus, 46, 49, 173, 187–88
Globe amaranth, 21, 177, 188
Globe mallow, 133, 150
Globe thistle, 50, 188
Globeflower, 188
Gloriosa daisy, 50, 188
Glory-of-the-snow, 188
Gloxinia, 188
Glue, 74, 79–82, 84, 90, 92, 151, 160, 168, 170, 171, 174, 178, 183
    dilution process for, 80–81
Glycerine, 14, 97–100, 102–6, 119, 171
Godetia, 61, 188
Golden chain, 188
Golden glow, 188
Golden rain, 104, 188
Goldenrod, 20–21, 56, 133–34
Gourds, 108
Grape, 104, 107
Grape hyacinth, 188
Grasses, 20, 21, 100, 119, 141
Great Salt Lake (oolitic) sand, 10, 19, 23–25, 28, 31–34
Greece, 2
Gum arabic, 144–45, 150, 152

Harry Lauder's Walking Stick, 89
Hawthorn, 106, 189

Heather, 20, 189
Hedge mustard, 134
Helichrysum, 21
Hemlock, 106
Hen-and-chickens, 189
Herbs, 107, 109–13
Hibiscus, 189
Holly, 12, 99, 106
Hollyhock, 38, 45, 68, 91, 154, 189
  color in, 49–51
  double, 45, 60, 161
  wild, 121, 134
Honesty, 20, 21, 189
Honey locust, 104
Honeysuckle, 189
Horse chestnut, 189
Horsetail, 141
Hyacinth, 134, 150, 189
  grape, 188
Hydrangea, 49–51, 104, 189
Hypericum, 190

Impatiens, 190
India, 3, 48, 162
Indian paintbrush, 123, 134–35
Indian rice, 141
Insects, 85, 124–25, 128, 130
Iris, 190
  foliage preservation of, 104
  German, 47, 170, 190
  white, 51
Ivy, 106

Jacaranda, 104
Japanese quince, 106
Job's tears, 21
Jonquil, 190
Juniper, 105

Kale, 108
Kerria, 190

Lace flower, 50, 190
Lamb's ears, 100, 104
Larkspur, 45, 49–51, 61, 70, 89, 190
Laurel, 104
Lavender, 109, 190
Leather fern, 102–4
Leatherleaf, 104
Leaves, *see* Foliage
Lemon, 104, 106
Lemon lily, 50
Leopard lily, 135
Lewisia, 135, 190
Lichen, 119
Lilacs, 38, 40, 45, 50, 51, 106, 190
  cutting of, 52
Lilies, 190–91
  blackberry, 180

calla, 51, 181
day, 46, 185
lemon, 50
leopard, 135
sand, 139
sego, 51, 117, 139–40
spray preserved of, 106
water, 49, 51, 52, 60, 105, 161, 191
Lily of the valley, 26, 46, 150, 191
  foliage preserved of, 104
  legend about, 1–2
Liquitex Matte Varnish, 151
Lobelia, 50, 191
Locoweed, 135
Locust
  black, 191
  honey, 104
Lovage, 109
Love-in-a-mist, 50, 191
Lupine, 104, 135
Lythrum, 50, 192

Magnolia, 104, 106, 192
Maidenhair fern, 102–4, 127
Manzanita, 15, 90
Maple, 106
Marguerite, 104, 192
Marigolds, 40, 50, 60, 192
  African, 45, 85, 92
  double, 69
  pot, 181
Matrimony vine, 106
Milkweed, 135
Mint, 145
Mock orange, 43, 51, 69, 103, 106, 172, 192
Moisture test, 59, 170, 174
Moisture-proofing spray, 55, 61, 84, 86, 122, 133, 151, 160, 169, *see also specific plants*
Monkey flower, 136
Monkshood, 136
Morning glory, 136, 192
Moss rose, 26, 91, 192–93
Mosses, 15, 106, 119
Mother box, 42, 59, 63, 77, 79–80
Mountain ash, 105, 136
Mountain boxwood, 119
Mullein, 136
Museum displays, 11, 15–16, 55, 115, 122–23, 134, 141–42
Myrtle, 106
  crape, 49, 184

Narcissus, 51, 193
Nasturtium, 145, 172, 193

Oak, 105
Ocotillo, 20, 49, 137

# Index

Oleander, 31, 51, 193
Onions, 137, 193
Orange flowers, 50, 53
Orchard, 141
Orchid, 193
Oregon grape, 50, 105, 137, 193

Painted daisies, 49, 193
Paints, for candied fruits, 149–50, *see also* Dyeing and painting
Palm, 105
Pansies, 46, 50, 194
Papyrus, 105
Parsley, 108
Passionflower, 194
Peach blossom, 177–78
Pelargonium, 172, 187
Penny-cress, 141
Pentstemons, 50, 121, 137, 194
Peonies, 45, 49, 51, 61, 172, 194
  candied, 146
  on Chinese tree, 15
  cutting of, 52
  foliage of, 99, 105
Petals
  in borax method, 22, 28–30
  of cacti, 123, 126
  falling off of, 170, 172, 174
  flexibility of, 28–30
  with Flower Sculpture Formula, 151
  glueing on, 79, 81, 84, 168
  in handling preserved flowers, 77, 155
  reinforcement for, 80–82, 168, 170, 171, 174, 178, 183
  in sand method, 23
  in silica gel method, 23
  texture of, *see* Texture
  transparency in, 47, 170, 172
Petunia, 48, 51, 54, 194
Phlox, 50, 137–38, 150, 194
  creeping, 122
Pine, 105
Pine cones, 119
Pinks, 90, 185
Plum blossom, 177–78
Poinsettia, 49, 173, 194
Polymer Medium, 91–92
Poppies, 138, 181, 195
Portulaca, 46, 195
Potato plants, 107–8
Prickly pear, 123–27
Primrose, 195
  evening, 46, 50, 122, 131
Prince's-feather, 195
Pumpkin flowers, 108
Pussy willow, 20, 138, 172

Queen Anne's lace, 51, 138

Quince blossom, 177–78

Ranunculus, 105, 195
*Readers' Digest, The,* 8
Red-hot poker, 195
Rhododendron, 105, 195
Rockrose, 189
Roman Empire, 2
Rosa hugonis, 43, 45, 101, 106
Rose acacia, 198
Rose of Sharon, 46, 50, 198
Roses, 25, 38, 86, 171, 195–97
  for beginners, 45
  Christmas, 182
  colors of, 48–51, 171, 196
  containers for, 39, 40
  in decoration, 13
  dyeing of, 49, 60
  in Egyptian tombs, 2
  Elsie Poulsen, 45
  in fifteenth century, 3
  Floradora, 49
  foliage of, 99
  Peace, 171
  reinforcement of, 171, 196
  Shah Jehan's wife and, 3
  single, 45, 68, 196
  Spalding's, 138
  spray preserved of, 106
  stems of, 66, 94–95
  tea, 45, 49, 196–97
  Tropicana, 49
  water for, 51
  wild, 116, 121, 123, 139

Sage, 109, 139, 140
  scarlet, 49, 198
Salpiglossis, 198
Sand, 18, 176
  amount needed of, 37–38, 62–63, 66–67
  in ancient times, 3
  borax-and-sand method with, 21–22, 176
  in cleaning flowers, 86
  drying of, 35, 75
  in face-down position, 70–71
  in face-up position, 66–69, 192
  in foliage preservation, 97, 99–106
  hand technique for, 63–65, 67–69, 72, 73
  mother box for, 42, 59, 63, 77, 79–80
  oolitic (Great Salt Lake), 23–25, 28, 30–34
  in restoration of old flowers, 160
  sifting of, 35–36
  in sure-fire moisture test, 59
  teachers' manual on, 164–65
  as therapeutic, 9–10

# Index

treatment for, 36–37
  in Victorian times, 4
  washing of, 33–35
  for wild plants, 119
Sand lily, 139
Sawdust, 18
Scabiosa, 50, 198
Schizanthus, 198
Scillia, 198
Sedum, 20, 198
Seed pods, 6, 20, 119
Sego lily, 51, 117, 139–40
Sepals, 83, 85, 92
Shadow boxes, 11, 13, 14
Shah Jehan's wife, 3
Sheen, 32, 37
  dyeing and, 46, 61, 92, 123, 187, 191
Shells, 119
Silica gel, 18, 22–23, 28–30, 32, 66
  color and, 23, 31
  for damp weather, 86
  drying time in, 23, 28, 75, 176
  in sand treatment, 37
Silver-lace vine, 198
Smilax, 106
Smoke tree, 198
Snapdragon, 49, 198
Snow Foam Products, Inc., 81
Snowball, 51, 105, 106, 198
Snowdrop, 51, 198
Snow-on-the-mountain, 105
Spiraea, 106, 161, 199
Sprays, 43, 69–75, 92, 103, 105–6, 172, 173, 177
Spruce, 105
Squirrel-tail, 141
Stamens, 60, 84, 117, 119, 177
  of cacti, 124, 126
Statice sinuata, 21
Steaming, 21, 90, 176, 184
Steershead bleeding heart, 140
Stems, 40, 79, 88–95
  chalk dusting for, 54
  curving of, 43, 89–90, 95, 102–155
  cutting of, 65–66, 88–89, 94–95
  in face-down covering, 70
  in face-up position, 66–67
  for foliage, 101–2
  in handling flowers, 77, 81
  in hang and dry method, 20–21
  of inverted cup flowers, 69
  in joining to flowers, 92–95, 174
  of long sprays, 74
  manzanita for, 90
  paint for, 90–92, 94, 168–69
  preparation of, 89
  of small flowers, 69, 88, 90
  steaming for, 21, 90
  for storage uses, 79, 88

teachers' manual on, 168
  of wild plants, 117, 119–22
  wire for, 88, 90, 92, 168, 171
  See also specific flowers
Stock, 49, 50, 199
Straw flowers, 20
Strawberries, 107, 109–10, 141
Sugar, 18
Sunflower, 140
Sweet alyssum, 69, 199
Sweet peas, 50, 140, 199
Sweet sultan, 199
Sweet William, 199
Sweetbrier (eglantine), 105, 186

Talcum powder, 18
  for flowers, 46, 54, 184, 185, 194, 195
  for foliage and stems, 128, 138, 140, 179, 194, 200
  on nectar, 130
Tamarisk, 20, 106, 199
Teasel, 140
Teculi, 2
Tertiary butyl alcohol method, 25–26, 179, 180, 185, 191, 193
Texture, 32, 46, 47, 171–72
  changes in, 54, 115, 172
  dyeing and, 49, 54, 86, 123, 134, 171–72
Thalictrum, 103, 105, 106
Thistle, 50, 140, 188
Tigridia, 199
Tomato leaves, 107
Topiary trees, 14–15
Tradescantia, 46, 50, 199
Tropical flowers, 173, 177
Trumpet creeper, 199
Tulip, 45, 50, 51, 200

Unicorn plant, 200
United States Forest Service, 15, 115

Vaughn Seed Company, 21
Vegetable foliage, 107–9
Verbena, 200
Veronica, 200
Viola, 200
Violet, 50, 69, 90, 105, 140–41, 200
  African, 176
  candied, 145, 146
  dogtooth, 131

Wandering Jew, 106
Washing powder, 18
Water lilies, 49, 51, 52, 60, 105, 161, 191
Water poppy, 200
Weeds, 6, 20

# Index

Weeping trees, 106
Weigela, 200
White flowers, 22, 26, 46, 50–51, 57, 123
Wild Flower Preservation Society, 116
Wild flowers and plants, 114–42, 176
  bell-shaped, 121
  cleaning of, 121–22
  covering, 119, 121
  cutting of, 52, 116–17, 119, 127
  dyeing of, 56, 119, 122–23
  in entirety, 120–21
  in flower shows, 16
  foliage of, 119, 121–23
  identification of, 117–18
  laws protecting, 117, 127
  list of, 127–42
  materials needed for, 52, 118–19
  moisture-proofing of, 122
  mounting of, 141–42

in museum collections, 11, 15–16, 55, 115, 122–23, 134, 141–42
notes on, 119
preservation of, 116–23
roots of, 117, 120
sprays of, 121
stems of, 117, 119–22
uncovering, 119, 121
water solution for, 52, 118–19
*See also specific flower*
Williamsburg, Virginia, 11, 19
Wisteria, 200

Xeranthemum, 21
Xochiquetzel, 1

Yarrow, 20, 56, 105, 141, 200
Yew, 105
Yucca, 105, 141

Zinnia, 49, 50, 54, 60, 86, 92, 171–72, 200